Workshop on Multiword Expressions: Identifying and Exploiting Underlying Properties 2006

Held in conjunction with COLING/ACL 2006

Sydney, Australia
23 July 2006

ISBN: 978-1-61738-504-9

Printed from e-media with permission by:

Curran Associates, Inc.
57 Morehouse Lane
Red Hook, NY 12571
www.proceedings.com

Some format issues inherent in the e-media version may also appear in this print version.

Printed by Curran Associates, Inc. (2010)

Association for Computational Linguistics
209 N. Eighth Street
Stroudsburg, Pennsylvania 18360

Phone: 1-570-476-8006
Fax: 1-570-476-0860

acl@aclweb.org

Table of Contents

Preface

This volume contains the papers accepted for presentation at the *Workshop on Multiword Expressions: Identifying and Exploiting Underlying Properties*. The workshop is endorsed by the Association for Computational Linguistics Special Interest Group on the Lexicon (SIGLEX) and is hosted in conjunction with the COLING/ACL 2006 on July 23rd, 2006 in Sydney, Australia.

There has been a growing awareness in the NLP community of the problems that multiword expressions (MWEs) pose. Developments in areas such as machine translation, text summarization, paraphrasing, grammar development and parsing, information retrieval, and question answering (to mention a few) have acknowledged difficulties due to the idiosyncratic nature of multiword expressions. This workshop continues a tradition of ACL workshops on Collocations (2001) and Multiword Expressions (2003 and 2004). Its specific objective is to focus on the underlying properties of MWEs. The call for papers expressed our interest in several topics such as the definition of MWEs, properties of MWEs and their impact on NLP applications, representation and treatment of the different classes of MWEs, linguistic and psycholinguistic analyses of MWEs, evaluation of extraction techniques and the importance of (non-)compositionality.

We received 23 submissions in total. Each submission was reviewed by (at least) three members of the program committee who not only judged each submission but also gave detailed comments to the authors. Among the received papers, 10 were selected for presentation at the workshop. After 3 papers have been withdrawn by their authors, seven papers are included in these proceedings.

The intention of this workshop is to focus on some fundamental questions on the nature of MWEs. To do this we will allow plenty of time for discussion to pursue some of the interesting, open and difficult questions that MWEs raise. As well as a discussion period after each session of papers, we will be organising group discussions at the end of the workshop. These will focus on problems of defining, characterising and evaluating MWEs, given what we know about the range of phenomena that they encompass as well as any important questions that have arisen during the workshop.

We would like to thank all the authors for submitting their research and the members of the program committee for their careful reviews and useful suggestions to the authors. We are indebted to Timothy Baldwin who will give an invited talk at the workshop. We would also like to thank the COLING/ACL 2006 organising committee that made this workshop possible and SIGLEX for agreeing to endorse this workshop. Finally, we hope that this workshop will provide food for thought for all participants.

Begoña Villada Moirón
Aline Villavicencio
Diana McCarthy
Stefan Evert
Suzanne Stevenson
June 2006

Organizers

Chairs:

Begoña Villada Moirón, University of Groningen (The Netherlands)
Aline Villavicencio, Federal University of Rio Grande do Sul (Brazil)
Diana McCarthy, University of Sussex (UK)
Stefan Evert, University of Osnabrueck (Germany)
Suzanne Stevenson, University of Toronto (Canada)

Program Committee:

Timothy Baldwin, Stanford University (USA); Melbourne University (Australia)
Colin Bannard, University of Edinburgh (UK)
Francis Bond, NTT Communication Science Laboratories (Japan)
Gosse Bouma, University of Groningen (The Netherlands)
Beatrice Daille, Nantes University (France)
Gael Dias, Beira Interior University (Portugal)
James Dowdall, University of Sussex (UK)
Afsaneh Fazly, University of Toronto (Canada)
Christiane Fellbaum, Princeton University (USA)
Nicole Gregoire, Utrecht University (The Netherlands)
Matthew Hurst, Inteliseek (USA)
Nancy Ide, Vassar College (USA)
Aravind Joshi, University of Pennsylvania (USA)
Kyo Kageura, National Institute of Informatics (Japan)
Anna Korhonen, University of Cambridge (UK)
Brigitte Krenn, OFAI, Vienna (Austria)
Mirella Lapata, University of Edinburgh (UK)
Roger Levy, University of Edinburgh (UK)
Rosamund Moon, University of Birmingham (UK)
Stephan Oepen, Stanford University (USA); University of Oslo (Norway)
Kentaro Ogura, NTT Cyber Space Laboratories (Japan)
Darren Pearce, London Knowledge Lab, (UK)
Scott Piao, University of Lancaster (UK)
Ivan Sag, University of Stanford (USA)
Violeta Seretan, University of Geneva (Switzerland)
Beata Trawinski, University of Tuebingen (Germany)
Kiyoko Uchiyama, Keio University (Japan)
Tom Wasow, Stanford University (USA)
Annie Zaenen, PARC (USA)

Invited Speaker:

Timothy Baldwin, Melbourne University (Australia)

Workshop Program

Sunday, 23 July 2006

9:15–9:30 Opening Remarks

9:30–10:30 *Compositionality and Multiword Expressions: Six of One, Half a Dozen of the Other?*
Timothy Baldwin (*Invited Speaker*)

10:30–11:00 Coffee break

Session 1: Compositionality and its Applications

11:00–11:30 *Measuring MWE Compositionality Using Semantic Annotation*
Scott S.L. Piao, Paul Rayson, Olga Mudraya, Andrew Wilson and Roger Garside

11:30–12:00 *Automatic Identification of Non-Compositional Multi-Word Expressions using Latent Semantic Analysis*
Graham Katz and Eugenie Giesbrecht

12:00–12:30 *Using Information about Multi-word Expressions for the Word-Alignment Task*
Sriram Venkatapathy and Aravind K. Joshi

12:30–12:45 Discussion

12:45–14:15 Lunch break

Session 2: Identification

14:15–14:45 *Detecting Complex Predicates in Hindi using POS Projection across Parallel Corpora*
Amitabha Mukerjee, Ankit Soni and Achla M Raina

14:45–15:15 *Automated Multiword Expression Prediction for Grammar Engineering*
Yi Zhang, Valia Kordoni, Aline Villavicencio and Marco Idiart

15:15–15:30 Discussion

15:30–16:00 Coffee break

Sunday, 23 July 2006 (continued)

Session 3: Classes and Underlying Semantics

16:00–16:30	*Classifying Particle Semantics in English Verb-Particle Constructions* Paul Cook and Suzanne Stevenson
16:30–17:00	*Interpretation of Compound Nominalisations using Corpus and Web Statistics* Jeremy Nicholson and Timothy Baldwin
17:00–17:15	Discussion
17:15–17:45	Group discussions
17:45–18:15	Summaries from group discussions
18:15	Closing Remarks

Compositionality and Multiword Expressions: Six of One, Half a Dozen of the Other?

Timothy Baldwin
Melbourne University

In this talk, I will investigate the relationship between compositionality and multiword expressions, as part of which I will outline different approaches for formalising the notion of compositionality. I will then briefly review computational methods that have been proposed for modelling compositionality, and applications thereof. Finally, I will discuss possible future directions for modelling compositionality, and present some preliminary results.

Proceedings of the Workshop on Multiword Expressions: Identifying and Exploiting Underlying Properties, page 1,
Sydney, July 2006.

Measuring MWE Compositionality Using Semantic Annotation

Scott S. L. Piao[1], Paul Rayson[1], Olga Mudraya[2], Andrew Wilson[2] and Roger Garside[1]

[1]Computing Department
Lancaster University
Lancaster, UK
{s.piao, p.rayson, r.garside}@lancaster.ac.uk

[2]Dept. of Linguistics and EL
Lancaster University
Lancaster, UK
{o.mudraya, a.wilson}@lancaster.ac.uk

Abstract

This paper reports on an experiment in which we explore a new approach to the automatic measurement of multi-word expression (MWE) compositionality. We propose an algorithm which ranks MWEs by their compositionality relative to a semantic field taxonomy based on the Lancaster English semantic lexicon (Piao et al., 2005a). The semantic information provided by the lexicon is used for measuring the semantic distance between a MWE and its constituent words. The algorithm is evaluated both on 89 manually ranked MWEs and on McCarthy et al's (2003) manually ranked phrasal verbs. We compared the output of our tool with human judgments using Spearman's rank-order correlation coefficient. Our evaluation shows that the automatic ranking of the majority of our test data (86.52%) has strong to moderate correlation with the manual ranking while wide discrepancy is found for a small number of MWEs. Our algorithm also obtained a correlation of 0.3544 with manual ranking on McCarthy et al's test data, which is comparable or better than most of the measures they tested. This experiment demonstrates that a semantic lexicon can assist in MWE compositionality measurement in addition to statistical algorithms.

1 Introduction

Over the past few years, compositionality and decomposability of MWEs have become important issues in NLP research. Lin (1999) argues that "non-compositional expressions need to be treated differently than other phrases in many statistical or corpus–based NLP methods". Compositionality means that "the meaning of the whole can be strictly predicted from the meaning of the parts" (Manning & Schütze, 2000). On the other hand, decomposability is a metric of the degree to which the meaning of a MWE can be assigned to its parts (Nunberg, 1994; Riehemann, 2001; Sag et al., 2002). These two concepts are closely related. Venkatapathy and Joshi (2005) suggest that "an expression is likely to be relatively more compositional if it is decomposable".

While there exist various definitions for MWEs, they are generally defined as cohesive lexemes that cross word boundaries (Sag et al., 2002; Copestake et al., 2002; Calzolari et al., 2002; Baldwin et al., 2003), which include nominal compounds, phrasal verbs, idioms, collocations etc. Compositionality is a critical criterion cutting across different definitions for extracting and classifying MWEs. While semantics of certain types of MWEs are non-compositional, like idioms "kick the bucket" and "hot dog", some others can have highly compositional semantics like the expressions "traffic light" and "audio tape".

Automatic measurement of MWE compositionality can have a number of applications. One of the often quoted applications is for machine translation (Melamed, 1997; Hwang & Sasaki, 2005), in which non-compositional MWEs need special treatment. For instance, the translation of a highly compositional MWE can possibly be inferred from the translations of its constituent words, whereas it is impossible for non-compositional MWEs, for which we need to identify the translation equivalent for the MWEs as a whole.

In this paper, we explore a new method of automatically estimating the compositionality of MWEs using lexical semantic information, sourced from the Lancaster semantic lexicon (Piao et al., 2005a) that is employed in the USAS[1] tagger (Rayson et al., 2004). This is a

[1] UCREL Semantic Analysis System

Proceedings of the Workshop on Multiword Expressions: Identifying and Exploiting Underlying Properties, pages 2–11,
Sydney, July 2006. ©2006 Association for Computational Linguistics

large lexical resource which contains nearly 55,000 single-word entries and over 18,800 MWE entries. In this lexicon, each MWE[2] and the words it contains are mapped to their potential semantic categories using a semantic field taxonomy of 232 categories. An evaluation of lexical coverage on the BNC corpus showed that the lexical coverage of this lexicon reaches 98.49% for modern English (Piao et al., 2004). Such a large-scale semantic lexical resource allows us to examine the semantics of many MWEs and their constituent words conveniently without resorting to large corpus data. Our experiment demonstrates that such a lexical resource provides an additional approach for automatically estimating the compositionality of MWEs.

One may question the necessity of measuring compositionality of manually selected MWEs. The truth is, even if the semantic lexicon under consideration was compiled manually, it does not exclusively consist of non-compositional MWEs like idioms. Built for practical discourse analysis, it contains many MWEs which are highly compositional but depict certain entities or semantic concepts. This research forms part of a larger effort to extend lexical resources for semantic tagging. Techniques are described elsewhere (e.g. Piao et al., 2005b) for finding new candidate MWE from corpora. The next stage of the work is to semi-automatically classify these candidates using an existing semantic field taxonomy and, to assist this task, we need to investigate patterns of compositionality.

2 Related Work

In recent years, various approaches have been proposed to the analysis of MWE compositionality. Many of the suggested approaches employ statistical algorithms.

One of the earliest studies in this area was reported by Lin (1999) who assumes that "non-compositional phrases have a significantly different mutual information value than the phrases that are similar to their literal meanings" and proposed to identify non-compositional MWEs in a corpus based on distributional characteristics of MWEs. Bannard et al. (2003) tested techniques using statistical models to infer the meaning of verb-particle constructions (VPCs), focusing on prepositional particles. They tested four methods over four compositional classification tasks, reporting that, on all tasks, at least one of the four methods offers an improvement in precision over the baseline they used.

McCarthy et al. (2003) suggested that compositional phrasal verbs should have similar neighbours as for their simplex verbs. They tested various measures using the nearest neighbours of phrasal verbs and their simplex counterparts, and reported that some of the measures produced results which show significant correlation with human judgments. Baldwin et al. (2003) proposed a LSA-based model for measuring the decomposability of MWEs by examining the similarity between them and their constituent words, with higher similarity indicating the greater decomposability. They evaluated their model on English noun-noun compounds and verb-particles by examining the correlation of the results with similarities and hyponymy values in WordNet. They reported that the LSA technique performs better on the low-frequency items than on more frequent items. Venkatapathy and Joshi (2005) measured relative compositionality of collocations having verb-noun pattern using a SVM (Support Vector Machine) based ranking function. They integrated seven various collocational and contextual features using their ranking function, and evaluated it against manually ranked test data. They reported that the SVM based method produces significantly better results compared to methods based on individual features.

The approaches mentioned above invariably depend on a variety of statistical contextual information extracted from large corpus data. Inevitably, such statistical information can be affected by various uncontrollable "noise", and hence there is a limitation to purely statistical approaches.

In this paper, we contend that a manually compiled semantic lexical resource can have an important part to play in measuring the compositionality of MWEs. While any approach based on a specific lexical resource may lack generality, it can complement purely statistical approaches by importing human expert knowledge into the process. Particularly, if such a resource has a high lexical coverage, which is true in our case, it becomes much more useful for dealing with general English. It should be emphasized that we propose our semantic lexical-based approach not as a substitute for the statistical approaches.

[2] In this lexicon, many MWEs are encoded as templates, such as *driv*_* {Np/P*/J*/R*} mad_JJ*, which represent variational forms of a single MWE, For further details, see Rayson et al., 2004.

Rather we propose it as a potential complement to them.

In the following sections, we describe our experiment and explore this approach to the issue of automatic estimation of MWE compositionality.

3 Measuring MWE compositionality with semantic field information

In this section, we propose an algorithm for automatically measuring MWE compositionality based on the Lancaster semantic lexicon. In this lexicon, the semantic field of each word and MWE is encoded in the form of semantic tags. We contend that the compositionality of a MWE can be estimated by measuring the distance between semantic fields of an MWE and its constituent words based on the semantic field information available from the lexicon.

The lexicon employs a taxonomy containing 21 major semantic fields which are further divided into 232 sub-categories.[3] Tags are designed to denote the semantic fields using letters and digits. For instance, tag *N3.2* denotes the category of {*SIZE*} and Q4.1 denotes {*media: Newspapers*}. Each entry in the lexicon maps a word or MWE to its potential semantic field category/ies. More often than not, a lexical item is mapped to multiple semantic categories, reflecting its potential multiple senses. In such cases, the tags are arranged by the order of likelihood of meanings, with the most prominent one at the head of the list. For example, the word "mass" is mapped to tags *N5*, *N3.5*, *S9*, *S5* and *B2*, which denote its potential semantic fields of {*QUANTITIES*}, {*MEASUREMENT: WEIGHT*}, {*RELIGION AND SUPERNATURAL*}, {*GROUPS AND AFFILIATION*} and {*HEALTH AND DISEASE*}.

The lexicon provides direct access to the semantic field information for large number of MWEs and their constituent words. Furthermore, the lexicon was analysed and classified manually by a team of linguists based on the analysis of corpus data and consultation of printed and electronic corpus-based dictionaries, ensuring a high level of consistency and accuracy of the semantic analysis.

In our context, we interpret the task of measuring the compositionality of MWEs as examining the distance between the semantic tag of a MWE and the semantic tags of its constituent words. Given a MWE M and its constituent words w_i ($i = 1, .., n$), the compositionality D can be measured by multiplying the semantic distance SD between M and each of its constituent words w_i. In practice, the square root of the product is used as the score in order to reduce the range of actual D-scores, as shown below:

$$(1)\quad D(M) = \sqrt{\prod_{i=1}^{n} SD(M, w_i)}$$

where D-score ranges between [0, 1], with 1 indicating the strongest compositionality and 0 the weakest compositionality.

In the semantic lexicon, as the semantic information of function words is limited, they are classified into a single grammatical bin (denoted by tag Z5). In our algorithm, they are excluded from the measuring process by using a stop word list. Therefore, only the content constituent words are involved in measuring the compositionality. Although function words may form an important part of many MWEs, such as phrasal verbs, because our algorithm solely relies on semantic field information, we assume they can be ignored.

The semantic distance between a MWE and any of its constituent words is calculated by quantifying the similarity between their semantic field categories. In detail, if the MWE and a constituent word do not share any of the major 21 semantic domains, the SD is assigned a small value λ.[4] If they do, three possible cases are considered:

Case a. If they share the same tag, and the constituent word has only one tag, then SD is one.

Case b. If they share a tag or tags, but the constituent words have multiple candidate tags, then SD is weighted using a variable α based on the position of the matched tag in the candidate list as well as the number of candidate tags.

Case c. If they share a major category, but their tags fall into different sub-categories (denoted by the trailing digits following a letter), SD is further weighted using a

[3] For the complete semantic tagset, see website: http://www.comp.lancs.ac.uk/ucrel/usas/

[4] We avoid using zero here in order to avoid producing semantic distance of zero indiscriminately when any one of the constituent words produces zero distance regardless of other constituent words.

variable β which reflects the difference of the sub-categories.

With respect to weight α, suppose L is the number of candidate tags of the constituent word under consideration, N is the position of the specific tag in the candidate list (the position starts from the top with N=1), then the weight α is calculated as

$$(2)\quad \alpha = \frac{L - N + 1}{L^2},$$

where N=1, 2, …, n and N<=L. Ranging between [1, 0), α takes into account both the location of the matched tag in the candidate tag list and the number of candidate tags. This weight penalises the words having more candidate semantic tags by giving a lower value for their higher degree of ambiguity. As either L or N increases, the α-value decreases.

Regarding the case c), where the tags share the same head letter but different digit codes, i.e. they are from the same major category but in different sub-categories, the weight β is calculated based on the number of sub-categories they share. As we mentioned earlier, a semantic tag consists of an initial letter and some trailing digits divided by points, e.g. *S1.1.2 {RECIPROCITY}*, *S1.1.3 {PARTICIPATION}*, *S1.1.4 {DESERVE}* etc. If we let T_1, T_2 be a pair of semantic tags with the same initial letters, which have k_i and k_j trailing digit codes (denoting the number of sub-division layers) respectively and share n digit codes from the left, or from the top layer, then β is calculated as follows:

$$(3)\quad \beta = \frac{n}{k};$$

$$(4)\quad k = \max(k_i, k_j).$$

where β ranges between (0, 1). In fact, the current USAS taxonomy allows only the maximum three layers of sub-division, therefore β has one of three possible scores: 0.500 (1/2), 0.333 (1/3) and 0.666 (2/3). In order to avoid producing zero scores, if the pair of tags do not share any digit codes except the head letter, then n is given a small value of 0.5.

Combining all of the weighting scores, the semantic distance *SD* in formula (1) is calculated as follows:

$$(5)\quad SD(M, w_i) = \begin{cases} \text{if no tag matches, then } \lambda; \\ \text{if a), then } 1; \\ \text{if b), then } \prod_{i=1}^{n} \alpha_i; \\ \text{if c), then } \prod_{i=1}^{n} \alpha_i \beta_i. \end{cases}$$

where λ is given a small value of 0.001 for our experiment[5].

Some MWEs and single words in the lexicon are assigned with combined semantic categories which are considered to be inseparable, as shown below:

petrol_NN1 station_NN1   M3/H1

where the slash means that this MWE falls under the categories of M3 *{VEHICLES AND TRANSPORTS ON LAND}* and H1 *{ARCHITECTURE AND KINDS OF HOUSES AND BUILDINGS}* at the same time. For such cases, criss-cross comparisons between all possible tag pairs are carried out in order to find the optimal match between the tags of the MWE and its constituent words.

By way of further explanation, the word "brush" as a verb has candidate semantic tags of *B4 {CLEANING AND PERSONAL CARE}* and *A1.1.1 {GENERAL ACTION, MAKING}* etc. On the other hand, the phrasal verb "brush down" may fall under either B4 category with the sense of *cleaning* or G2.2 category *{ETHICS}* with the sense of *reprimand*. When we apply our algorithm to it, we get the *D*-score of 1.0000 for the sense of *cleaning*, indicating a high degree of compositionality, whereas we get a low *D*-score of 0.0032 for the sense of *reprimand*, indicating a low degree of compositionality. Note that the word "down" in this MWE is filtered out as it is a functional word.

The above example has only a single constituent content word. In practice, many MWEs have more complex structures than this example. In order to test the performance of our algorithm, we compared its output against human judgments of compositionality, as reported in the following section.

4 Manually Ranking MWEs for Evaluation

In order to evaluate the performance of our tool against human judgment, we prepared a list

[5] As long as λ is small enough, it does not affect the ranking of *D*-scores.

of 89 MWEs[6] and asked human raters to rank them via a website. The list includes six MWEs with multiple senses, and these were treated as separate MWE. The Lancaster MWE lexicon has been compiled manually by expert linguists, therefore we assume that every item in this lexicon is a true MWE, although we acknowledge that some errors may exist.

Following McCarthy et al.'s approach, we asked the human raters to assign each MWE a number ranging between 0 (opaque) and 10 (fully compositional). Both native and non-native speakers are involved, but only the data from native speakers are used in this evaluation. As a result, three groups of raters were involved in the experiment. Group 1 (6 people) rated MWEs with indexes of 1-30, Group 2 (4 people) rated MWEs with indexes of 31-59 and Group 3 (five people) rated MWEs with indexes of 6-89.

In order to test the level of agreement between the raters, we used the procedures provided in the 'irr' package for R (Gamer, 2005). With this tool, the average intraclass correlation coefficient (ICC) was calculated for each group of raters using a two-way agreement model (Shrout & Fleiss, 1979). As a result, all ICCs exceeded 0.7 and were significant at the 95% confidence level, indicating an acceptable level of agreement between raters. For Group 1, the ICC was 0.894 (95% ci = 0.807 < ICC < 0.948), for Group 2 it was 0.9 (95% ci=0.783<ICC<0.956) and for Group 3 it was 0.886 (95% ci = 0.762 < ICC < 0.948).

Based on this test, we conclude that the manual ranking of the MWEs is reliable and is suitable to be used in our evaluation. Source data for the human judgements is available from our website in spreadsheet form[7].

5 Evaluation

In our evaluation, we focused on testing the performance of the *D*-score against human raters' judgment on ranking different MWEs by their degree of compositionality, as well as distinguishing the different degrees of compositionality for each sense in the case of multiple tags.

The first step of the evaluation was to implement the algorithm in a program and run the tool on the 89 test MWEs we prepared. Fig. 1 illustrates the *D*-score distribution in a bar chart. As shown by the chart, the algorithm produces a widely dispersed distribution of *D*-scores across the sample MWEs, ranging from 0.000032 to 1.000000. For example, the tool assigned the score of 1.0 to the *FOOD* sense and 0.001 to the THIEF senses of "tea leaf" successfully distinguishing the different degrees of compositionality of these two senses.

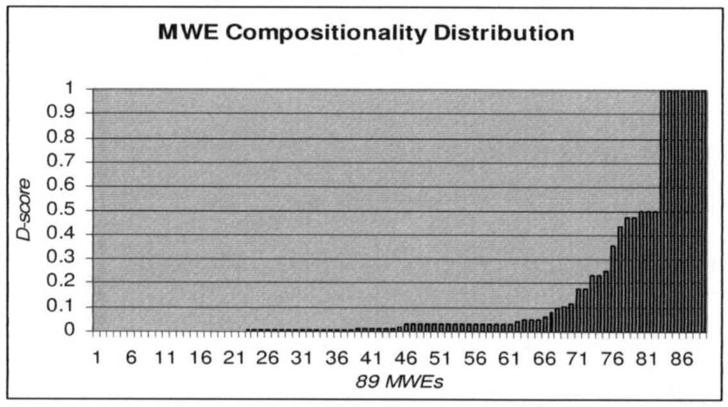

Fig 1: *D*-score distribution across 89 sample MWEs

As shown in Fig. 1, some MWEs share the same scores, reflecting the limitation of the number of ranks that our algorithm can produce as well as the limited amount of semantic information available from a lexicon. Nonetheless, the algorithm produced 45 different scores which ranked the MWEs into 45 groups (see the steps in the figure). Compared to the eleven scores used by the human raters, this provides a fine-grained ranking of the compositionality.

The primary issue in our evaluation is the extent to which the automatic ranking of the MWEs correlates with the manual ranking of them. As described in the previous section, we created a list of 89 manually ranked MWEs for this purpose. Since we are mainly interested in the ranks rather than the actual scores, we examined the correlation between the automatic and manual rankings using Spearman's correlation coefficient. (For the full ranking list, see Appendix).

In the manually created list, each MWE was ranked by 3-6 human raters. In order to create a unified single test data of human ranking, we calculated the average of the human ranks for each MWE. For example, if two human raters give ranks 3 and 4 to a MWE, then its rank is (3+4)/2=3.5. Next, the MWEs are sorted by the averaged ranks in descending order to obtain the combined ranks of the MWEs. Finally, we sorted the MWEs by the *D*-score in the same way to obtain a parallel list of automatic ranks. For the calculation of Spearman's correlation coefficient, if *n* MWEs are tied to a score (either *D*-score or the average manual ranks), their ranks were ad-

[6] Selected at random from the Lancaster semantic lexicon.
[7] http://ucrel.lancs.ac.uk/projects/assist/

justed by dividing the sum of their ranks by the number of MWEs involved. Fig. 2 illustrates the correspondence between the adjusted automatic and manual rankings.

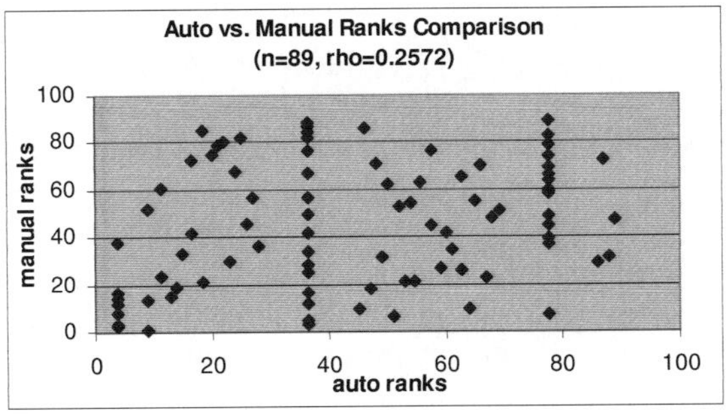

Fig. 2: Scatterplot of automatic *vs.* manual ranking.

As shown in Fig. 2, the overall correlation seems quite weak. In the automatic ranking, quite a few MWEs are tied up to three ranks, illustrated by the vertically aligned points. The precise correlation between the automatic and manual rankings was calculated using the function provided in R for Windows 2.2.1. Spearman's rank correlation (*rho*) for these data was 0.2572 (p=0.01495), indicating a significant though rather weak positive relationship.

In order to find the factors causing this weak correlation, we tested the correlation for those MWEs whose rank differences were less than 20, 30, 40 and 50 respectively. We are interested to find out how many of them fall under each of the categories and which of their features affected the performance of the algorithm. As a result, we found 43, 54, 66 and 77 MWEs fall under these categories respectively, which yield different correlation scores, as shown in Table 1.

numb of MWEs	Percent (%)	Rank diff	*rho*-score	Sig.
43	48.31	<20	0.9149	*P<0.001*
54	60.67	<30	0.8321	*P<0.001*
66	74.16	<40	0.7016	*P<0.001*
77	86.52	<50	0.5084	*P<0.001*
89 (total)	100.00	<=73	0.2572	*P<0.02*

Table 1: Correlation coefficients corresponding different rank differences.

As we expected, the *rho* decreases as the rank difference increases, but all of the four categories containing a total of 77 MWEs (86.52%) show reasonably high correlations, with the minimum score of 0.5084. [8] In particular, 66 of them (74.16%), whose ranking differences are less than 40, demonstrate a strong correlation with rho-score 0.7016, as illustrated by Fig. 3

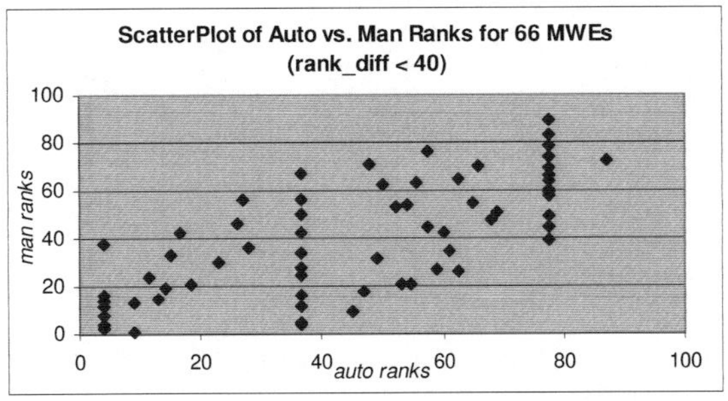

Fig 3: ScatterPlot for 66 MWEs (rank_diff < 40) which shows a strong correlation

Our manual examination shows that the algorithm generally pushes the highly compositional and non-compositional MWEs towards opposite ends of the spectrum of the *D*-score. For example, those assigned with score 1 include "aid worker", "audio tape" and "unemployment figure". On the other hand, MWEs such as "tea leaf" (meaning thief), "kick the bucket" and "hot dog" are given a low score of 0.001. We assume these two groups of MWEs are generally treated as highly compositional and opaque MWEs respectively.

However, the algorithm could be improved. A major problem found is that the algorithm punishes longer MWEs which contain function words. For example, "make an appearance" is scored 0.000114 by the algorithm, but when the article "an" is removed, it gets a higher score 0.003608. Similarly, when the preposition "up" is removed from "keep up appearances", it gets 0.014907 compared to the original 0.000471, which would push up their rank much higher. To address this problem, the algorithm needs to be refined to minimise the impact of the function words to the scoring process.

Our analysis also reveals that 12 MWEs with rank differences (between automatic and manual ranking) greater than 30 results in a degraded overall correlation. Table 2 lists these words, in which the higher ranks indicate higher compositionality.

[8] Salkind (2004: 88) suggests that *r*-score ranges 0.4~0.6, 0.6~0.8 and 0.8~1.0 indicate moderate, strong and very strong correlations respectively.

MWE	Sem. Tag[9]	Auto rank	Manual rank
plough into	A9-	53.5	3
Bloody Mary	F2	53.5	2
pillow fight	K6	26	80.5
lollipop lady	M3/S2	70	15
cradle snatcher	S3.2/T3/S2	73.5	17.5
go bananas	X5.2+++	65	8.5
make an appearance	S1.1.3+	2	58.5
keep up appearances	A8/S1.1.1	4	61
sandwich course	P1	69	11.5
go bananas	B2-/X1	68	10
Eskimo roll	M4	71.5	5
in other words	Z4	12.5	83

Table 2: Twelve MWEs having rank differences greater than 50.

Let us take "pillow fight" as an example. The whole expression is given the semantic tag K6, whereas neither "pillow" nor "fight" as individual word is given this tag. In the lexicon, "pillow" is classified as H5 {*FURNITURE AND HOUSEHOLD FITTINGS*} and "fight" is assigned to four semantic categories including S8- {*HINDERING*}, X8+ {*HELPING*}, E3- {*VIOLENT/ANGRY*}, and K5.1 {*SPORTS*}. For this reason, the automatic score of this MWE is as low as 0.003953 on the scale of [0, 1]. On the contrary, human raters judged the meaning of this expression to be fairly transparent, giving it a high score of 8.5 on the scale of [0, 10]. Similar contrasts occurred with the majority of the MWEs with rank differences greater than 50, which are responsible for weakening the overall correlation.

Another interesting case we noticed is the MWE "pass away". This MWE has two major senses in the semantic lexicon L1- {*DIE*} and T2- {*END*} which were ranked separately. Remarkably, they were ranked in the opposite order by human raters and the algorithm. Human raters felt that the sense *DIE* is less idiomatic, or more compositional, than *END*, while the algorithm indicated otherwise. The explanation of this again lies in the semantic classification of the lexicon, where "pass" as a single word contains the sense T2- but not L1-. Consequently, the automatic score for "pass away" with the sense L1- is much lower (0.001) than that with the sense of T2- (0.007071).

In order to evaluate our algorithm in comparison with previous work, we also tested it on the manual ranking list created by McCarthy et al (2003).[10] We found that 79 of the 116 phrasal verbs in that list are included in the Lancaster semantic lexicon. We applied our algorithm on those 79 items to compare the automatic ranks against the average manual ranks using the Spearman's rank correlation coefficient (*rho*). As a result, we obtained $rho=0.3544$ with significance level of $p=0.001357$. This result is comparable with or better than most measures reported by McCarthy et al (2003).

6 Discussion

The algorithm we propose in this paper is different from previous proposed statistical methods in that it employs a semantic lexical resource in which the semantic field information is directly accessible for both MWEs and their constituent words. Often, typical statistical algorithms measure the semantic distance between MWEs and their constituent words by comparing their contexts comprising co-occurrence words in near context extracted from large corpora, such as Baldwin et al's algorithm (2003).

When we consider the definition of the compositionality as the extent to which the meaning of the MWE can be guessed based on that of its constituent words, a semantic lexical resource which maps MWEs and words to their semantic features provides a practical way of measuring the MWE compositionality. The Lancaster semantic lexicon is one such lexical resource which allows us to have direct access to semantic field information of large number of MWE and single words. Our experiment demonstrates the potential value of such semantic lexical resources for the automatic measurement of MWE compositionality. Compared to statistical algorithms which can be affected by a variety of uncontrollable factors, such as size and domain of corpora, etc., an expert-compiled semantic lexical resource can provide much more reliable and "clean" lexical semantic information.

However, we do not suggest that algorithms based on semantic lexical resources can substitute corpus-based statistical algorithms. Rather, we suggest it as a complement to existing statistical algorithms. As the errors of our algorithm

[9] Semantic tags occurring in Table 2: A8 (seem), A9 (giving possession), B2 (health and disease), F2 (drink), K6 (children's games and toys), M3 (land transport), M4 (swimming), P1 (education), S1.1.1 (social actions), S1.1.3 (participation), S2 (people), S3.2 (relationship), T3 (time: age), X1 (psychological actions), X5.2 (excited), Z4 (discourse bin)

[10] This list is available at website: http://mwe.stanford.edu/resources/

reveal, the semantic information provided by the lexicon alone may not be rich enough for a very fine-grained distinction of MWE compositionality. In order to obtain better results, this algorithm needs to be combined with statistical techniques.

A limitation of our approach is language-dependency. In order to port our algorithm to languages other than English, one needs to build similar semantic lexicon in those languages. However, similar semantic lexical resources are already under construction for some other languages, including Finnish and Russian (Löfberg et al., 2005; Sharoff et al., 2006), which will allow us to port our algorithm to those languages.

7 Conclusion

In this paper, we explored an algorithm based on a semantic lexicon for automatically measuring the compositionality of MWEs. In our evaluation, the output of this algorithm showed moderate correlation with a manual ranking. We claim that semantic lexical resources provide another approach for automatically measuring MWE compositionality in addition to the existing statistical algorithms. Although our results are not yet conclusive due to the moderate scale of the test data, our evaluation demonstrates the potential of lexicon-based approaches for the task of compositional analysis. We foresee, by combining our approach with statistical algorithms, that further improvement can be expected.

8 Acknowledgement

The work reported in this paper was carried out within the UK-EPSRC-funded ASSIST Project (Ref. EP/C004574).

References

Timothy Baldwin, Colin Bannard, Takaaki Tanaka, and Dominic Widdows. 2003. An Empirical Model of Multiword Expression Compositionality. In *Proc. of the ACL 2003 Workshop on Multiword Expressions: Analysis, Acquisition and Treatment*, pages 89-96, Sapporo, Japan.

Colin Bannard, Timothy Baldwin, and Alex Lascarides. 2003. A statistical approach to the semantics of verb-particles. In *Proc. of the ACL2003 Workshop on Multiword Expressions: Analysis, Acquisition and Treatment*, pages 65–72, Sapporo.

Nicoletta Calzolari, Charles Fillmore, Ralph Grishman, Nancy Ide, Alessandro Lenci, Catherine MacLeod, and Antonio Zampolli. 2002. Towards best practice for multiword expressions in computational lexicons. In *Proc. of the Third International Conference on Language Resources and Evaluation (LREC 2002)*, pages 1934–1940, Las Palmas, Canary Islands.

Ann Copestake, Fabre Lambeau, Aline Villavicencio, Francis Bond, Timothy Baldwin, Ivan A. Sag, and Dan Flickinger. 2002. Multiword expressions: Linguistic precision and reusability. In *Proc. of the Third International Conference on Language Resources and Evaluation (LREC 2002)*, pages 1941–1947, Las Palmas, Canary Islands.

Matthias Gamer. 2005. The irr Package: Various Coefficients of Interrater Reliability and Agreement. Version 0.61 of 11 October 2005. Available from: cran.r-project.org/src/contrib/Descriptions/irr.html

Dekang Lin. 1999. Automatic identification of non-compositional phrases. In *Proc. of the 37th Annual Meeting of the ACL*, pages 317–324, College Park, USA.

Laura Löfberg, Scott Piao, Paul Rayson, Jukka-Pekka Juntunen, Asko Nykänen, and Krista Varantola. 2005. A semantic tagger for the Finnish language. In *Proc. of the Corpus Linguistics 2005 conference*, Birmingham, UK.

Christopher D. Manning and Hinrich Schütze. 2000. *Foundations of Statistical Natural Language Processing*. The MIT Press, Cambridge, Massachusetts.

Diana McCarthy, Bill Keller, and John Carroll. 2003. Detecting a continuum of compositionality in phrasal verbs. In *Proc. of the ACL-2003 Workshop on Multiword Expressions: Analysis, Acquisition and Treatment*, pages 73–80, Sapporo, Japan.

Dan Melamed. 1997. Automatic discovery of non-compositional compounds in parallel data. In *Proc. of the 2nd Conference on Empirical Methods in Natural Language Processing* , Providence, USA.

Geoffrey Nunberg, Ivan A. Sag, and Tom Wasow. 1994. Idioms. *Language*, 70: 491–538.

Scott S.L. Piao, Paul Rayson, Dawn Archer and Tony McEnery. 2004. Evaluating Lexical Resources for a Semantic Tagger. In *Proc. of LREC-04*, pages 499–502, Lisbon, Portugal.

Scott S.L. Piao, Dawn Archer, Olga Mudraya, Paul Rayson, Roger Garside, Tony McEnery and Andrew Wilson. 2005a. A Large Semantic Lexicon for Corpus Annotation. In *Proc. of the Corpus Linguistics Conference 2005*, Birmingham, UK.

Scott S.L. Piao., Paul Rayson, Dawn Archer, Tony McEnery. 2005b. Comparing and combining a semantic tagger and a statistical tool for MWE extraction. *Computer Speech and Language*, 19, 4: 378–397.

Paul Rayson, Dawn Archer, Scott Piao, and Tony McEnery. 2004. The UCREL Semantic Analysis System. In *Proc. of LREC-04 Workshop: Beyond Named Entity Recognition Semantic Labeling for NLP Tasks*, pages 7–12, Lisbon, Portugal.

Susanne Riehemann. 2001. *A Constructional Approach to Idioms and Word Formation*. Ph.D. thesis, Stanford University, Stanford.

Ivan A. Sag, Timothy Baldwin, Francis Bond, Ann Copestake, and Dan Flickinger. 2002. Multiword Expressions: A Pain in the Neck for NLP. In *Proc. of the 3rd International Conference on Intelligent Text Processing and Computational Linguistics (CICLing-2002)*, pages 1–15, Mexico City, Mexico.

Neil J. Salkind. 2004. Statistics for People Who Hate Statistics. Sage: Thousand Oakes, US.

Serge Sharoff, Bogdan Babych, Paul Rayson, Olga Mudraya and Scott Piao. 2006. ASSIST: Automated semantic assistance for translators. Proceedings of EACL 2006, pages 139–142, Trento, Italy.

Patrick E. Shrout and Joseph L. Fleiss. 1979. Intraclass Correlations: Uses in Assessing Rater Reliability. Psychological Bulletin (2), 420–428.

Sriram Venkatapathy and Aravind K. Joshi. 2005. Measuring the relative compositionality of verb-noun (V-N) collocations by integrating features. In *Proc. of Human Language Technology Conference and Conference on Empirical Methods in Natural Language Processing (HLT/EMNLP 2005)*, pages 899–906, Vancouver, Canada.

Appendix: Manual *vs*. Automatic Ranks of Sample MWEs

The table below shows the human and automatic rankings of 89 sample MWEs. The MWEs are sorted in ascending order by manual average ranks. The top items are supposed to be the most compositional ones. For example, according to the manual ranking, facial expression is the most compositional MWE while tea leaf is the most opaque one. This table also shows that some MWEs are tied up with the same ranks. For the definitions of the full semantic tagset, see website http://www.comp.lancs.ac.uk/ucrel/usas/.

MWE Tag	Sem tag	Man rank	Auto. rank
facial expression	B1	1	9
aid worker	S8/S2	2	4
audio tape	K3	3.5	4
leisure activities	K1	3.5	36.5
advance warning	T4/Q2.2	5	36.5
living space	H2	6	51
in other words	Z4	7	77.5
unemployment figures	I3.1/N5	8	4
camera angle	Q4.3	9.5	45
pillow fight	K6	9.5	64
youth club	S5/T3	11.5	4
petrol station	M3/H1	11.5	36.5
palm tree	L3	13	9
rule book	G2.1/Q4.1	14	4
ball boy	K5.1/S2.2	15	13
goal keeper	K5.1/S2	16.5	4
kick in	E3-	16.5	36.5
ventilation shaft	H2	18	47
directory enquiries	Q1.3	19	14
phone box	Q1.3/H1	21	18.5
lose balance	M1	21	53
bend the rules	A1.7	21	54.5
big nose	X7/X2.4	23	67
quantity control	N5/A1.7	24	11.5
act of God	S9	25	36.5
air bag	A15/M3	26	62.5
mind stretching	A12	27	59
plain clothes	B5	28	36.5
keep up appearances	A8/S1.1.1	29	86
examining board	P1	30	23
open mind	X6	31.5	49
make an appearance	S1.1.3+	31.5	88
cable television	Q4.3	33	15
king size	N3.2	34	36.5
action point	X7	35	61
keep tight rein on	A1.7	36	28
noughts and crosses	K5.2	37	77.5
tea leaf	L3/F2	38	4
single minded	X5.1	39.5	77.5
window dressing	I2.2	39.5	77.5
street girl	G1.2/S5	42	36.5
just over the horizon	S3.2/S2.1	42	60
pressure group	T1.1.3	42	16.5
air proof	O4.1	44.5	57.5
heart of gold	S1.2.2	44.5	77.5
lose heart	X5.2	46	26
food for thought	X2.1/X5.1	47	89
play part	S8	48	68
look down on	S1.2.3	49	77.5
arm twisting	Q2.2	50	36.5
take into account	A1.8	51	69
kidney bean	F1	52	9
come alive	A3+	53	52
break new ground	T3/T2	54	54
make up to	S1.1.2	55	65
by virtue of	C1	56.5	36.5
snap shot	A2.2	56.5	27
pass away	L1-	58	77.5
long face	E4.1	59	77.5
bossy boots	S1.2.3/S2	60	77.5
plough into	M1/A1.1.2	61	11.5
kick in	T2+	62	50
animal magnetism	S1.2	63	55.5
sixth former	P1/S2	64	77.5
pull the strings	S7.1	65	62.5
couch potato	A1.1.1/S2	66	77.5
think tank	S5/X2.1	67	36.5
come alive	X5.2+	68	24
hot dog	F1	69	77.5
cheap shot	G2.2-/Q2.2	70	66

rock and roll	K2	71	48
bright as a button	S3.2/T3/S2	72.5	87
cradle snatcher	X9.1+	72.5	16.5
alpha wave	B1	74	77.5
lollipop lady	M3/S2	75	20
pass away	X5.2+	76.5	57.5
plough into	T2-	76.5	36.5
piece of cake	P1	78.5	77.5
sandwich course	A12	78.5	21
go bananas	B2-/X1	80	22
go bananas	X5.2+++	81.5	36.5
go bananas	E3-	81.5	25
kick the bucket	L1	83	77.5
on the wagon	F2	84	36.5
Eskimo roll	M4	85	18.5
acid house	K2	86	46
plough into	A9-	87	36.5
Bloody Mary	F2	88	36.5
tea leaf	G2.1-/S2mf	89	77.5

Automatic Identification of Non-Compositional Multi-Word Expressions using Latent Semantic Analysis

Graham Katz
Institute of Cognitive Science
University of Osnabrück
gkatz@uos.de

Eugenie Giesbrecht
Institute of Cognitive Science
University of Osnabrück
egiesbre@uos.de

Abstract

Making use of latent semantic analysis, we explore the hypothesis that local linguistic context can serve to identify multi-word expressions that have non-compositional meanings. We propose that vector-similarity between distribution vectors associated with an MWE as a whole and those associated with its constitutent parts can serve as a good measure of the degree to which the MWE is compositional. We present experiments that show that low (cosine) similarity does, in fact, correlate with non-compositionality.

1 Introduction

Identifying non-compositional (or idiomatic) multi-word expressions (MWEs) is an important subtask for any computational system (Sag et al., 2002), and significant attention has been paid to practical methods for solving this problem in recent years (Lin, 1999; Baldwin et al., 2003; Villada Moirón and Tiedemann, 2006). While corpus-based techniques for identifying collocational multi-word expressions by exploiting statistical properties of the co-occurrence of the component words have become increasingly sophisticated (Evert and Krenn, 2001; Evert, 2004), it is well known that mere co-occurrence does not well distinguish compositional from non-compositional expressions (Manning and Schütze, 1999, Ch. 5).

While expressions which may potentially have idiomatic meanings can be identified using various lexical association measures (Evert and Krenn, 2001; Evert and Kermes, 2003), other techniques must be used to determining whether or not a particular MWE does, in fact, have an idiomatic use. In this paper we explore the hypothesis that the local linguistic context can provide adequate cues for making this determination and propose one method for doing this.

We characterize our task on analogy with word-sense disambiguation (Schütze, 1998; Ide and Véronis, 1998). As noted by Schütze, WSD involves two related tasks: the general task of sense discrimination—determining what senses a given word has—and the more specific task of sense selection—determining for a particular use of the word in context which sense was intended. For us the discrimination task involves determining for a given expression whether it has a non-compositional interpretation in addition to its compositional interpretation, and the selection task involves determining in a given context, whether a given expression is being used compositionally or non-compostionally. The German expression *ins Wasser fallen*, for example, has a non-compositional interpretation on which it means 'to fail to happen' (as in (1)) and a compositional interpretation on which it means 'to fall into water (as in (2)).[1]

(1) *Das Kind war beim Baden von einer Luftmatratze ins Wasser gefallen.*
'The child had fallen into the water from an a air matress while swimming'

(2) *Die Eröffnung des Skateparks ist ins Wasser gefallen.*
'The opening of the skatepark was cancelled'

The discrimination task, then, is to identify *ins Wasser fallen* as an MWE that has an idiomatic meaning and the selection task is to determine that

[1]Examples taken from a newspaper corpus of the German Süddeutsche Zeitung (1994-2000)

Proceedings of the Workshop on Multiword Expressions: Identifying and Exploiting Underlying Properties, pages 12–19, Sydney, July 2006. ©2006 Association for Computational Linguistics

in (1) it is the compositional meaning that is intended, while in (2) it is the non-compositional meaning.

Following Schütze (1998) and Landauer & Dumais (1997) our general assumption is that the meaning of an expression can be modelled in terms of the words that it co-occurs with: its co-occurrence signature. To determine whether a phrase has a non-compositional meaning we compute whether the co-occurrence signature of the phrase is systematically related to the co-occurrence signatures of its parts. Our hypothesis is that a systematic relationship is indicative of compositional interpretation and lack of a systematic relationship is symptomatic of non-compositionality. In other words, we expect compositional MWEs to appear in contexts more similar to those in which their component words appear than do non-compositional MWEs.

In this paper we describe two experiments that test this hypothesis. In the first experiment we seek to confirm that the local context of a known idiom can reliably distinguish idiomatic uses from non-idiomatic uses. In the second experiment we attempt to determine whether the difference between the contexts in which an MWE appears and the contexts in which its component words appear can indeed serve to tell us whether the MWE has an idiomatic use.

In our experiments we make use of lexical semantic analysis (LSA) as a model of context-similarity (Deerwester et al., 1990). Since this technique is often used to model meaning, we will speak in terms of "meaning" similiarity. It should be clear, however, that we are only using the LSA vectors—derived from context of occurrence in a corpus—to model meaning and meaning composition in a very rough way. Our hope is simply that this rough model is sufficient to the task of identifying non-compositional MWEs.

2 Previous work

Recent work which attempts to discriminate between compositional and non-compositional MWEs include Lin (1999), who used mutual-information measures identify such phrases, Baldwin et al. (2003), who compare the distribution of the head of the MWE with the distribution of the entire MWE, and Vallada Moirón & Tiedemann (2006), who use a word-alignment strategy to identify non-compositional MWEs making use of parallel texts. Schone & Jurafsky (2001) applied LSA to MWE identification, althought they did not focus on distinguishing compositional from non-compositional MWEs.

Lin's goal, like ours, was to discriminate non-compositional MWEs from compositional MWEs. His method was to compare the mutual information measure of the constituents parts of an MWE with the mutual information of similar expressions obtained by substituting one of the constituents with a related word obtained by thesaurus lookup. The hope was that a significant difference between these measures, as in the case of *red tape* (mutual information: 5.87) compared to *yellow tape* (3.75) or *orange tape* (2.64), would be characteristic of non-compositional MWEs. Although intuitively appealing, Lin's algorithm only achieves precision and recall of 15.7% and 13.7%, respectively (as compared to a gold standard generate from an idiom dictionary—but see below for discussion).

Schone & Jurafsky (2001) evaluated a number of co-occurrence-based metrics for identifying MWEs, showing that, as suggested by Lin's results, there was need for improvement in this area. Since LSA has been used in a number of meaning-related language tasks to good effect (Landauer and Dumais, 1997; Landauer and Psotka, 2000; Cederberg and Widdows, 2003), they had hoped to improve their results by identify non-compositional expressions using a method similar to that which we are exploring here. Although they do not demonstrate that this method actually identifies non-compositional expressions, they do show that the LSA similarity technique only improves MWE identification minimally.

Baldwin et al., (2003) focus more narrowly on distinguishing English noun-noun compounds and verb-particle constructions which are compositional from those which are not compositional. Their approach is methodologically similar to ours, in that they compute similarity on the basis of contexts of occurrance, making use of LSA. Their hypothesis is that high LSA-based similarity between the MWE and each of its constituent parts is indicative of compositionality. They evaluate their technique by assessing the correlation between high semantic similarity of the constituents of an MWE to the MWE as a whole with the likelihood that the MWE appears in WordNet as a hyponym of one of the constituents. While the expected correlation was not attested, we suspect this to be more an indication of the inappropriateness of the evaluation used than of the faultiness of the general approach.

Lin, Baldwin et al., and Schone & Jurafsky, all use as their gold standard either idiom dictionaries or WordNet (Fellbaum, 1998). While Schone & Jurafsky show that WordNet is as good a standard as any of a number of machine readable dictionaries, none of these authors shows that the MWEs that appear in WordNet (or in the MRDs) are generally non-compositional, in the relevant sense. As noted by Sag et al. (2002) many MWEs are simply "institutionalized phrases" whose meanings are perfectly compositional, but whose frequency of use (or other non-linguistic factors) make them highly salient. It is certainly clear that many MWEs that appear in WordNet—examples being *law student, medical student, college man*—are perfectly compositional semantically.

Zhai (1997), in an early attempt to apply statistical methods to the extraction of non-compositional MWEs, made use of what we take to be a more appropriate evaluation metric. In his comparison among a number of different heuristics for identifying non-compositional noun-noun compounds, Zhai did his evaluation by applying each heuristic to a corpus of items hand-classified as to their compositionality. Although Zhai's classification appears to be problematic, we take this to be the appropirate paradigm for evaluation in this domain, and we adopt it here.

3 Proceedure

In our work we made use of the Word Space model of (semantic) similiarty (Schütze, 1998) and extended it slightly to MWEs. In this framework, "meaning" is modeled as an n-dimensional vector, derived via singular value decomposition (Deerwester et al., 1990) from word co-occurrence counts for the expression in question, a technique frequently referred to as *Latent Semantic Analysis* (LSA). This kind of dimensionality reduction has been shown to improve performance in a number of text-based domains (Berry et al., 1999).

For our experiments we used a local German newspaper corpus.[2] We built our LSA model with the Infomap Software package.[3], using the 1000 most frequent words not on the 102-word hand-generated stop list as the content-bearing dimension words (the columns of the matrix). The 20,000 most frequent content words were assigned row values by counting occurrences within a 30-word window. SVD was used to reduce the dimensionality from 1000 to 100, resulting in 100 dimensional "meaning"-vectors for each word. In our experiments, MWEs were assigned meaning-vectors as a whole, using the same proceedure. For meaning similarity we adopt the standard measure of cosine of the angle between two vectors (the normalized correlation coefficient) as a metric (Schütze, 1998; Baeza-Yates and Ribeiro-Neto, 1999). On this metric, two expressions are taken to be unrelated if their meaning vectors are orthogonal (the cosine is 0) and synonymous if their vectors are parallel (the cosine is 1).

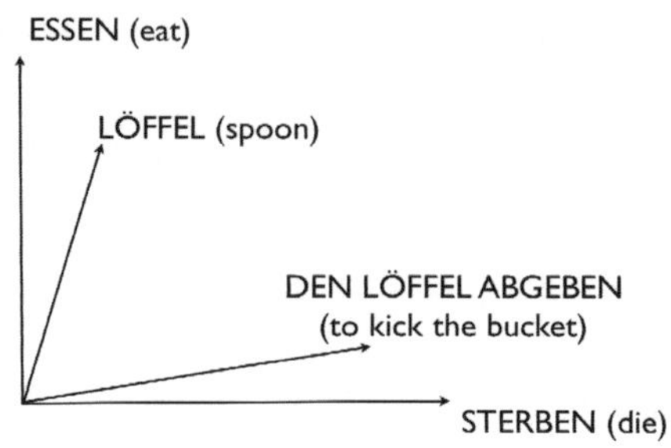

Figure 1: Two dimensional Word Space

Figure 1 illustrates such a vector space in two dimensions. Note that the meaning vector for *Löffel* 'spoon' is quite similar to that for *essen* 'to eat' but distant from *sterben* 'to die', while the meaning vector for the MWE *den Löffel abgeben* is close to that for *sterben*. Indeed *den Löffel abgeben*, like *to kick the bucket*, is a non-compositional idiom meaning 'to die'.

While *den Löffel abgeben* is used almost exclusively in its idiomatic sense (all four occurrences in our corpus), many MWEs are used regularly in both their idiomatic and in their literal senses. About two thirds of the uses of the MWE *ins Wasser fallen* in our corpus are idiomatic uses, and the remaing one third are literal uses. In our first experiment we tested the hypothesis that these uses could reliably be distinguished using distribution-based models of their meaning.

[2] Süddeutsche Zeitung (SZ) corpus for 2003 with about 42 million words.

[3] Available from `infomap.stanford.edu`.

3.1 Experiment I

For this experiment we manually annotated the 67 occurrences of *ins Wasser fallen* in our corpus as to whether the expression was used compositionally (literally) or non-compositionally (idiomatically).[4] Marking this distinction we generate an LSA meaning vectors for the compositional uses and an LSA meaning vector for the non-compositional uses of *ins Wasser fallen*. The vectors turned out, as expected, to be almost orthogonal, with a cosine of the angle between them of 0.02. This result confirms that the linguistic contexts in which the literal and the idiomatic use of *ins Wasser fallen* appear are very different, indicating—not surprisingly—that the semantic difference between the literal meaning and the idiomatic meaning is reflected in the way these these phrases are used.

Our next task was to investigate whether this difference could be used in particular cases to determine what the intended use of an MWE in a particular context was. To evaluate this, we did a 10-fold cross-validation study, calculating the literal and idiomatic vectors for *ins Wasser fallen* on the basis of the training data and doing a simple nearest neighbor classification of each memember of the test set on the basis of the meaning vectors computed from its local context (the 30 word window). Our result of an average accurace of 72% for our LSA-based classifier far exceeds the simple maximum-likelihood baseline of 58%.

In the final part of this experiment we compared the meaning vector that was computed by summing over all uses of *ins Wasser fallen* with the literal and idiomatic vectors from above. Since idiomatic uses of *ins Wasser fallen* prevail in the corpus (2/3 vs. 1/3), it is not surprisingly that the similarity to the literal vector (0.0946) is much than similarity to the idiomatic vector (0.3712).

To summarize Experiment I, which is a variant of a supervised phrase sense disambiguation task, demonstrates that we can use LSA to distinguish between literal and the idiomatic usage of an MWE by using local linguistic context.

[4]This was a straightforward task; two annotators annotated independently, with very high agreement—kappa score of over 0.95 (Carletta, 1996). Occurrences on which the annotators disagreed were thrown out. Of the 64 occurrences we used, 37 were idiomatic and 27 were literal.

3.2 Experiment II

In our second experiment we sought to make use of the fact that there are typically clear distributional difference between compositional and non-compositional uses of MWEs to determine whether a given MWE indeed has non-compositional uses at all. In this experiment we made use of a test set of German Preposition-Noun-Verb "collocation candidate" database whose extraction is described by Krenn (2000) and which has been made available electronically.[5] From this database only word combinations with frequency of occurrence more than 30 in our test corpus were considered. Our task was to classify these 81 potential MWEs according whether or not thay have an idiomatic meaning.

To accomplish this task we took the following approach. We computed on the basis of the distribution of the components of the MWE an estimate for the compositional meaning vector for the MWE. We then compared this to the actual vector for the MWE as a whole, with the expectation MWEs which indeed have non-compositinoal uses will be distinguished by a relatively low vector similarity between the estimated compositional meaning vector and the actual meaning vector. In other words small similarity values should be diagnostic for the presense of non-compositinoal uses of the MWE.

We calculated the estimated compositional meaning vector by taking it to be the sum of the meaning vector of the parts, i.e., the compositional meaning of an expression $w1w2$ consisting of two words is taken to be sum of the meaning vectors for the constituent words.[6] In order to maximize the independent contribution of the constituent words, the meaning vectors for these words were always computed from contexts in which they appear alone (that is, not in the local context of the other constituent). We call the estimated compositional meaning vector the "composed" vector.[7]

The comparisons we made are illustrated in Figure 2, where vectors for the MWE *auf die Strecke bleiben* 'to fall by the wayside' and the words *Strecke* 'route' and *bleiben* 'to stay' are mapped

[5]Available as an example data collection in UCS-Toolkit 5 from `www.collocations.de`.

[6]For all our experiments we consider only two-word combinations.

[7]Schone & Jurafsky (2001) explore a few modest variations of this estimate.

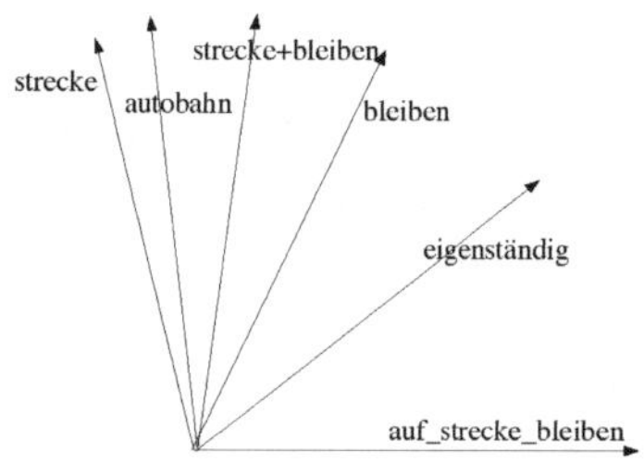

Figure 2: Composed versus Multi-Word

into two dimensions[8]. (the words *Autobahn* 'highway' and *eigenständig* 'independent' are given for comparison). Here we see that the linear combination of the component words of the MWE is clearly distinct from that of the MWE as a whole.

As a further illustration of the difference between the composed vector and the MWE vector, in Table 2 we list the words whose meaning vector is most similar to that of the MWE *auf dis Strecke bleiben* along with their similarity values, and in Table 3 we list those words whose meaning vector is most similar to the composed vector. The semantic differences among these two classes are readily apparent.

folgerung	'consequence'	0.769663
eigenständig	'independent'	0.732372
langfristiger	'long-term'	0.731411
herbeiführen	'to effect'	0.717294
ausnahmefälle	'exceptions'	0.704939

Table 1: **auf die Strecke bleiben**

strecken	'to lengthen'	0.743309
fahren	'to drive'	0.741059
laufen	'to run'	0.726631
fahrt	'drives'	0.712352
schließen	'to close'	0.704364

Table 2: **Strecke+bleiben**

We recognize that the composed vector is clearly nowhere near a perfect model of compositional meaning in the general case. This can be illustrated by considering, for example, the MWE *fire breathing*. This expression is clearly compositional, as it denotes the process of producing combusting exhalation, exactly what the semantic combination rules of the English would predict. Nevertheless the distribution of *fire breathing* is quite unrelated to that of its constituents *fire* and *breathing* (the former appears frequently with *dragon* and *circus* while the later appear frequently with *blaze* and *lungs*, respectively). Despite these principled objections, the composed vector provides a useful baseline for our investigation. We should note that a number of researchers in the LSA tradition have attempted to provide more compelling combinatory functions to capture the non-linearity of linguistic compositional interpretation (Kintsch, 2001; Widdows and Peters, 2003).

As a check we chose, at random, a number of simple clearly-compositional word combinations (not from the candidate MWE list). We expected that on the whole these would evidence a very high similarity measure when compared with their associated composed vector, and this is indeed the case, as shown in Table 1. We also compared the literal and non-literal vectors for *ins Wasser fallen* from the first experiment with the composed vector, computed out of the meaning vectors for *Wasser* and for *fallen*.[9] The difference isn't large, but nevertheless the composed vector is more similar to the literal vector (cosine of 0.2937) than to the non-literal vector (cosine of 0.1733).

vor Gericht verantworten 'to appear in court'	0.80735103
im Bett liegen 'to lie in bed'	0.76056000
aus Gefängnis entlassen 'dismiss from prison'	0.66532673

Table 3: Non-idiomatic phrases

Extending to the general case, our task was to compare the composed vector to the actual vector for all the MWEs in our test set. The resulting cosine similarity values range from 0.01 to 0.80. Our hope was that there would be a similarity threshold for distinguishing MWEs that have non-compositional interpretations from those that do not. Indeed of the MWEs with a similarity values of under 0.1, just over half are MWEs which were hand-annotated to have non-literal uses.[10] It

[8]The preposition *auf* and the article *die* are on the stop list

[9]The preposition *ins* is on the stop list and plays no role in the computation.

[10]The similarity scores for the entire test set are given in

is clear then that the technique described is, *prima facie*, capable of detecting idiomatic MWEs.

3.3 Evaluation and Discussion

To evaluate the method, we used the careful manual annotation of the PNV database described by Krenn (2000) as our gold standard. By adopting different threshholds for the classification decision, we obtained a range of results (trading off precision and recall). Table 4 illustrates this range.

The F-score measure is maximized in our experiments by adopting a similarity threshold of 0.2. This means that MWEs which have a meaning vector whose cosine is under this value when compared with with the combined vector should be classified as having a non-literal meaning.

To compare our method with that proposed by Baldwin et al. (2003), we applied their method to our materials, generating LSA vectors for the component content words in our candidate MWEs and comparing their semantic similarity to the MWEs LSA vector as a whole, with the expectation being that low similarity between the MWE as a whole and its component words is indication of the non-compositionality of the MWE. The results are given in Table 5.

It is clear that while Baldwin et al.'s expectation is borne out in the case of the constituent noun (the non-head), it is not in the case of the constituent verb (the head). Even in the case of the nouns, however, the results are, for the most part, markedly inferior to the results we achieved using the composed vectors.

There are a number of issues that complicate the workability of the unsupervised technique described here. We rely on there being enough non-compositional uses of an idiomatic MWE in the corpus that the overall meaning vector for the MWE reflects this usage. If the literal meaning is overwhelmingly frequent, this will reduce the effectivity of the method significantly. A second problem concerns the relationship between the literal and the non-literal meaning. Our technique relies on these meaning being highly distinct. If the meanings are similar, it is likely that local context will be inadequate to distinguish a compositional from a non-compositional use of the expression. In our investigation it became apparent, in fact, that in the newspaper genre, highly idiomatic expressions such as *ins Wasser fallen* were often used in their idiomatic sense (apparently for humorous effect) particularly frequently in contexts in which elements of the literal meaning were also present.[11]

Appendix I.

4 Conclusion

To summarize, in order to classify an MWE as non-compositional, we compute an approximation of its compositional meaning and compare this with the meaning of the expression as it is used on the whole. One of the obvious improvements to the algorithm could come from better models for simulating compositional meaning. A further issue that can be explored is whether linguistic preprocessing would influence the results. We worked only on raw text data. There is some evidence (Baldwin et al., 2003) that part of speech tagging might improve results in this kind of task. We also only considered local word sequences. Certainly some recognition of the syntactic structure would improve results. These are, however, more general issues associated with MWE processing.

Rather promising results were attained using only local context, however. Our study shows that the F-score measure is maximized by taking as threshold for distinguishing non-compositional phrases from compositional ones a cosine similarity value somewhere between 0.1-0.2. An important point to be explored is that compositionality appears to come in degrees. As Bannard and Lascarides (2003) have noted, MWEs "do not fall cleanly into the binary classes of compositional and non-compositional expressions, but populate a continuum between the two extremes." While our experiment was designed to classify MWEs, the technique described here, of course, provides a means, if rather a blunt one, for quantifying the degreee of compositonality of an expression.

References

Ricardo A. Baeza-Yates and Berthier A. Ribeiro-Neto. 1999. *Modern Information Retrieval*. ACM Press / Addison-Wesley.

Timothy Baldwin, Colin Bannard, Takaaki Tanaka, and Dominic Widdows. 2003. An empirical model

[11] One such example from the SZ corpus: *Der Auftakt wäre allerdings fast ins Wasser gefallen, weil ein geplatzter Hydrant eine fünfzehn Meter hohe Wasserfontäne in die Luft schleuderte.*
'The prelude almost didn't occur, because a burst hydrant shot a fifteen-meter high fountain into the sky.'

	cos < 0.1	cos < 0.2	cos < 0.3	cos < 0.4	cos < 0.5
Precision	0.53	0.39	0.29	0.22	0.21
Recall	0.42	0.63	0.84	0.89	0.95
F-measure	0.47	**0.48**	0.43	0.35	0.34

Table 4: Evaluation of Various Similarity Thresholds

	cos < 0.1	cos < 0.2	cos < 0.3	cos < 0.4	cos < 0.5
Verb F-measure	0.21	0.16	0.29	0.26	0.27
Noun F-measure	0.28	0.51	0.43	0.39	0.33

Table 5: Evaluation of Method of Baldwin et al. (2003)

of multiword expression decomposability. In *Proceedings of the ACL-2003 Workshop on Multiword Expressions: Analysis, Acquisition and Treatment*, pages 89–96, Sapporo, Japan.

Colin Bannard, Timothy Baldwin, and Alex Lascarides. 2003. A statistical approach to the semantics of verb-particles. In *Proceedings of the ACL-2003 Workshop on Multiword Expressions: Analysis, Acquisition and Treatment*, pages 65–72, Sapporo, Japan.

Michael W. Berry, Zlatko Drmavc, and Elisabeth R. Jessup. 1999. Matrices, vector spaces, and information retrieval. *SIAM Review*, 41(2):335–362.

Jean Carletta. 1996. Assessing agreement on classification tasks: The kappa statistic. *Computational Linguistics*, 22(2):249–254.

Scott Cederberg and Dominic Widdows. 2003. Using LSA and noun coordination information to improve the precision and recall of automatic hyponymy extraction. In *In Seventh Conference on Computational Natural Language Learning*, pages 111–118, Edmonton, Canada, June.

Scott C. Deerwester, Susan T. Dumais, Thomas K. Landauer, George W. Furnas, and Richard A. Harshman. 1990. Indexing by latent semantic analysis. *Journal of the American Society of Information Science*, 41(6):391–407.

Stefan Evert and Hannah Kermes. 2003. Experiments on candidate data for collocation extraction. In *Companion Volume to the Proceedings of the 10th Conference of The European Chapter of the Association for Computational Linguistics*, pages 83–86, Budapest, Hungary.

Stefan Evert and Brigitte Krenn. 2001. Methods for the qualitative evaluation of lexical association measures. In *Proceedings of the 39th Annual Meeting of the Association for Computational Linguistics*, pages 188–195, Toulouse, France.

Stefan Evert. 2004. *The Statistics of Word Cooccurrences: Word Pairs and Collocations*. Ph.D. thesis, University of Stuttgart.

Christiane Fellbaum. 1998. *WordNet, an electronic lexical database*. MIT Press, Cambridge, MA.

Nancy Ide and Jean Véronis. 1998. Word sense disambiguation: The state of the art. *Computational Linguistics*, 14(1).

Walter Kintsch. 2001. Predication. *Cognitive Science*, 25(2):173–202.

Brigitte Krenn. 2000. *The Usual Suspects: Data-Oriented Models for Identification and Representation of Lexical Collocations*. Dissertations in Computational Linguistics and Language Technology. German Research Center for Artificial Intelligence and Saarland University, Saarbrücken, Germany.

Thomas K. Landauer and Susan T. Dumais. 1997. A solution to plato's problem: The latent semantic analysis theory of the acquisition, induction, and representation of knowledge. *Psychological Review*, 104:211–240.

Thomas K. Landauer and Joseph Psotka. 2000. Simulating text understanding for educational applications with latent semantic analysis: Introduction to LSA. *Interactive Learning Environments*, 8(2):73–86.

Dekang Lin. 1999. Automatic identification of non-compositional phrases. In *Proceedings of the 37th Annual Meeting of the Association for Computational Linguistics*, pages 317–324, College Park, MD.

Christopher D. Manning and Hinrich Schütze. 1999. *Foundations of Statistical NaturalLanguage Processing*. The MIT Press, Cambridge, MA.

Ivan A. Sag, Timothy Baldwin, Francis Bond, Ann A. Copestake, and Dan Flickinger. 2002. Multiword expressions: A pain in the neck for NLP. In *Proceedings of the 3rd International Conferences on Intelligent Text Processing and Computational Linguistics*, pages 1–15.

Patrick Schone and Daniel Jurafsky. 2001. Is knowledge-free induction of multiword unit dictionary headwords a solved problem? In *Proceedings of Empirical Methods in Natural Language Processing*, Pittsburgh, PA.

Hinrich Schütze. 1998. Automatic word sense discrimination. *Computational Linguistics*, 24(1):97–124.

Begoña Villada Moirón and Jörg Tiedemann. 2006. Identifying idiomatic expressions using automatic word-alignment. In *Proceedings of the EACL 2006 Workshop on Multiword Expressions in a Multilingual Context*, Trento, Italy.

Dominic Widdows and Stanley Peters. 2003. Word vectors and quantum logic: Experiments with negation and disjunction. In *Eighth Mathematics of Language Conference*, pages 141–150, Bloomington, Indiana.

Chengxiang Zhai. 1997. Exploiting context to identify lexical atoms – a statistical view of linguistic context. In *Proceedings of the International and Interdisciplinary Conference on Modelling and Using Context (CONTEXT-97)*, pages 119–129.

APPENDIX

Similarity (cosine) values for the combined and the MWE vector. Uppercase entries are those hand-annotated as being MWEs which have an idiomatic interpretation.

Word Combinations	*Cosines*
(vor) gericht verantworten	0.80735103
(in) bett liegen	0.76056000
(aus) gefängnis entlassen	0.66532673
(zu) verfüung stellen	0.60310321
(aus) haft entlassen	0.59105617
(um) prozent steigern	0.55889772
(ZU) KASSE BITTEN	0.526331
(auf) prozent sinken	0.51281725
(IN) TASCHE GREIFEN	0.49350031
(zu) verfügung stehen	0.49236563
(auf) prozent steigen	0.47422122
(um) prozent zulegen	0.47329672
(in) betrieb gehen	0.47262171
(unter) druck geraten	0.44377297
(in) deutschland leben	0.44226071
(um) prozent steigen	0.41498688
(in) rechnung stellen	0.40985534
(von) prozent erreichen	0.39407666
(auf) markt kommen	0.38740534
(unter) druck setzen	0.37822936
(in) vergessenheit geraten	0.36654168
(um) prozent sinken	0.36600216
(in) rente gehen	0.36272313
(zu) einsatz kommen	0.3562527
(zu) schule gehen	0.35595884
(in) frage stellen	0.35406327
(in) frage kommen	0.34714701
(in) luft sprengen	0.34241143
(ZU) GESICHT BEKOMMEN	0.34160325
(vor) gericht ziehen	0.33405685
(in) gang setzen	0.33231573
(in) anspruch nehmen	0.32217044
(auf) prozent erhöhen	0.31574088
(um) prozent wachsen	0.3151615
(in) empfang nehmen	0.31420746
(für) sicherheit sorgen	0.30230156
(zu) ausdruck bringen	0.30001438
(IM) MITTELPUNKT STEHEN	0.29770654
(zu) ruhe kommen	0.29753093
(IM) AUGE BEHALTEN	0.2969367
(in) urlaub fahren	0.29627064
(in) kauf nehmen	0.2947628
(in) pflicht nehmen	0.29470704
(in) höhe treiben	0.29450525
(in) kraft treten	0.29311349
(zu) kenntnis nehmen	0.28969961
(an) start gehen	0.28315812
(auf) markt bringen	0.2800427
(in) ruhe standgehen	0.27575604
(bei) prozent liegen	0.27287073
(um) prozent senken	0.26506203
(UNTER) LUPE NEHMEN	0.2607078
(zu) zug kommen	0.25663165
(zu) ende bringen	0.25210009
(in) brand geraten	0.24819525
(ÜBER) BÜHNE GEHEN	0.24644366
(um) prozent erhöhen	0.24058016
(auf) tisch legen	0.23264335
(auf) bühne stehen	0.23136641
(auf) idee kommen	0.23097735
(zu) ende gehen	0.20237252
(auf) spiel setzen	0.20112171
(IM) VORDERGRUND STEHEN	0.18957473
(IN) LEERE LAUFEN	0.18390151
(zu) opfer fallen	0.17724105
(in) gefahr geraten	0.17454816
(in) angriff nehmen	0.1643926
(auer) kontrolle geraten	0.16212899
(IN) HAND NEHMEN	0.15916243
(in) szene setzen	0.15766861
(ZU) SEITE STEHEN	0.14135151
(zu) geltung kommen	0.13119923
(in) geschichte eingehen	0.12458956
(aus) ruhe bringen	0.10973377
(zu) fall bringen	0.10900036
(zu) wehr setzen	0.10652383
(in) griff bekommen	0.10359659
(auf) tisch liegen	0.10011075
(IN) LICHTER SCHEINEN	0.08507655
(zu) sprache kommen	0.08503791
(IM) STICH LASSEN	0.0735844
(unter) beweis stellen	0.06064519
(IM) WEG STEHEN	0.05174435
(AUS) FUGEN GERATEN	0.05103952
(in) erinnerung bleiben	0.04339438
(ZU) WORT KOMMEN	0.03808749
(AUF) STRAßE GEHEN	0.03492515
(AUF) STRECKE BLEIBEN	0.03463844
(auer) kraft setzen	0.0338813
(AUF) WEG BRINGEN	0.03122951
(zu) erfolg führen	0.02882997
(in) sicherheit bringen	0.02862914
(in) erfühlung gehen	0.01515792
(in) zeitung lesen	0.00354598

Using Information about Multi-word Expressions for the Word-Alignment Task

Sriram Venkatapathy[1]
Language Technologies Research Center,
Indian Institute of
Information Technology,
Hyderabad, India.
sriramv@linc.cis.upenn.edu

Aravind K. Joshi
Department of Computer and
Information Science and Institute for
Research in Cognitive Science,
University of Pennsylvania, PA, USA.
joshi@linc.cis.upenn.edu

Abstract

It is well known that multi-word expressions are problematic in natural language processing. In previous literature, it has been suggested that information about their degree of compositionality can be helpful in various applications but it has not been proven empirically. In this paper, we propose a framework in which information about the multi-word expressions can be used in the word-alignment task. We have shown that even simple features like point-wise mutual information are useful for word-alignment task in English-Hindi parallel corpora. The alignment error rate which we achieve (AER = 0.5040) is significantly better (about 10% decrease in AER) than the alignment error rates of the state-of-art models (Och and Ney, 2003) (Best AER = 0.5518) on the English-Hindi dataset.

1 Introduction

In this paper, we show that measures representing compositionality of multi-word expressions can be useful for tasks such as Machine Translation, word-alignment to be specific here. We use an online learning framework called MIRA (McDonald et al., 2005; Crammer and Singer, 2003) for training a discriminative model for the word alignment task (Taskar et al., 2005; Moore, 2005). The discriminative model makes use of features which represent the compositionality of multi-word expressions.

Multi-word expressions (MWEs) are those whose structure and meaning cannot be derived from their component words, as they occur independently. Examples include conjunctions such as '*as well as*' (meaning 'including'), idioms like '*kick the bucket*' (meaning 'die') phrasal verbs such as '*find out*' (meaning 'search') and compounds like '*village community*'. They can be defined roughly as idiosyncratic interpretations that cross word boundaries (Sag et al., 2002).

A large number of MWEs have standard syntactic structure but are semantically non-compositional. Here, we consider the class of verb based expressions (verb is the head of the phrase), which occur very frequently. This class of verb based multi-word expressions include verbal idioms, support-verb constructions, among others. The example '*take place*' is a MWE but '*take a gift*' is not.

In the past, various measures have been suggested for measuring the compositionality of multi-word expressions. Some of these are mutual information (Church and Hanks, 1989), distributed frequency (Tapanainen et al., 1998) and Latent Semantic Analysis (LSA) model (Baldwin et al., 2003). Even though, these measures have been shown to represent compositionality quite well, compositionality itself has not been shown to be useful in any application yet. In this paper, we explore this possibility of using the information about compositionality of MWEs (verb based) for the word alignment task. In this preliminary work, we use simple measures (such as point-wise mutual information) to measure compositionality.

The paper is organized as follows. In section 2, we discuss the word-alignment task with respect to the class of multi-word expressions of interest in this paper. In section 3, we show empirically,

[1]At present visiting Institute for Research in Cognitive Science, University of Pennsylvania, PA, USA.

Proceedings of the Workshop on Multiword Expressions: Identifying and Exploiting Underlying Properties, pages 20–27,
Sydney, July 2006.

the behavior of verb based expressions in a parallel corpus (English-Hindi in our case). We then discuss our alignment algorithm in section 4. In section 5, we describe the features which we have used in our training model. Section 6 discusses the training algorithm and in section 7, the results of our discriminative model for the word alignment task. Related work and conclusion follow in section 8 and 9 respectively.

2 Task: Word alignment of verbs and their dependents

The task is to align the verbs and their dependents (arguments and adjuncts) in the source language sentence (English) with words in the target language sentence (Hindi). The dependents of the verbs in the source sentence are represented by their head words. Figure 1. shows an example of the type of multi-word expressions which we consider for alignment.

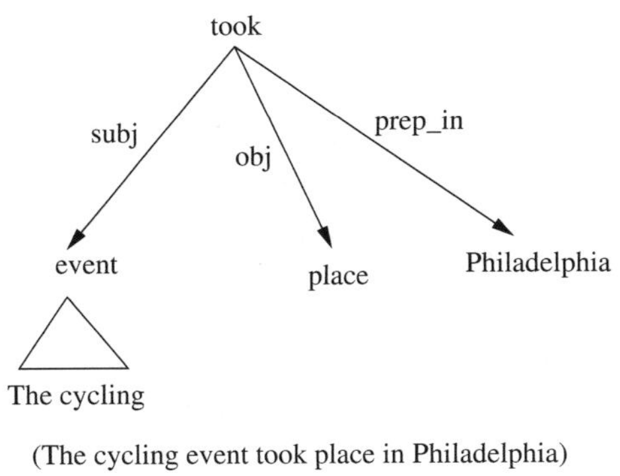

Figure 1: Example of MWEs we consider

In the above example, the goal will the to align the words 'took', 'event', 'place' and 'Philadelphia' with corresponding word(s) in the target language sentence (which is not parsed) using a discriminative approach. The advantage in using the discriminative approach for alignment is that it lets you use various compositionality based features which are crucial towards aligning these expressions. Figure 2. shows the appropriate alignment of the expression in Figure 1. with the words in the target language. The pair (take place), in English, a verb and one of its dependents is aligned with a single verbal unit in Hindi.

It is essential to obtain the syntactic roles for dependents in the source language sentence as they are required for computing the compositionality value between the dependents and their verbs. The

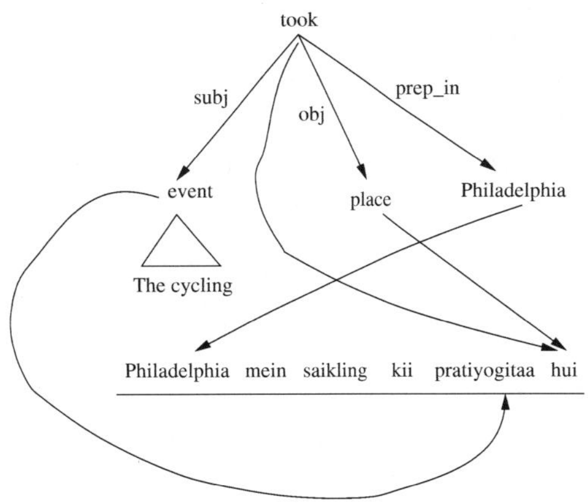

Figure 2: Alignment of Verb based expression

syntactic roles on the source side are obtained by applying simple rules to the output of a dependency parser. The dependency parser which we used in our experiments is a stochastic TAG based dependency parser (Shen, 2006). A sentence could have one or more verbs. We would like to align all the expressions represented by those verbs with words in the target language.

3 Behavior of MWEs in parallel corpora

In this section, we will briefly discuss the complexity of the alignment problem based on the verb based MWE's. From the word aligned sentence pairs, we compute the fraction of times a source sentence verb and its dependent are aligned together with the same word in the target language sentence. We count the number of times a source sentence verb and its dependent are aligned together with the same word in the target language sentence, and divide it by the total number of dependents. The total size of our word aligned corpus is 400 sentence pairs which includes both training and test sentences. The total number of dependents present in these sentences are 2209. Total number of verb dependent pairs which aligned with same word in target language are 193. Hence, the percentage of such occurrences is 9%, which is a significant number.

4 Alignment algorithm

In this section, we describe the algorithm for aligning verbs and their dependents in the source language sentence with the words in the target language. Let V be the number of verbs and A be the number of dependents. Let the number of words in the target language be N. If we explore all the ways in which the $V + A$ words in the source sentence are aligned with words in the target language before choosing the best alignment, the total number of possibilites are N^{V+A}. This is computationally very expensive. Hence, we use a Beam-search algorithm to obtain the K-best alignments.

Our algorithm has three main steps.

1. Populate the Beam : Use the local features (which largely capture the co-occurence information between the source word and the target word) to determine the K-best alignments of verbs and their dependents with words in the target language.

2. Re-order the Beam: Re-order the above alignments using more complex features (which include the global features and the compositionality based feature(s)).

3. Post-processing : Extend the alignment(s) of the verb(s) (on the source side) to include words which can be part of the verbal unit on the target side.

For a source sentence, let the verbs and dependents be denoted by s_{ij}. Here i is the index of the verb ($1 <= i <= V$). The variable j is the index of the dependents ($0 <= j <= A$) except when $j = 0$ which is used to represent the verb itself. Let the source sentences be denoted as $S = \{s_{ij}\}$ and the target sentences by $T = \{t_n\}$. The alignment from a source sentence S to target sentence T is defined as the mapping $\bar{a} = \{a_{ijn} \mid a_{ijn} \equiv (s_{ij} \rightarrow t_n), \forall i, j\}$. A beam is used to store a set of K-best alignments between a source sentence and the target sentence. It is represented using the symbol B where B_k ($0 <= k <= K$) is used to refer to a particular alignment configuration.

4.1 Populate the Beam

The task in this step is to obtain the K-best candidate alignments using local features. The local features mainly contain the coccurence information between a source and a target word and are independent of other alignment links or words in the sentences. Let the local feature vector be denoted as $f_L(s_{ij}, t_k)$. The score of a particular alignment link is computed by taking the dot product of the weight vector W with the local feature vector (of words connected by the alignment link). Hence, the local score will be

$$score_L(s_{ij}, t_k) = W.f_L(s_{ij}, t_k)$$

The total score of an alignment configuration is computed by adding the scores of individual links in the alignment configuration. Hence, the alignment score will be

$$score_{La}(\bar{a}, S, T) = \sum score_L(s_{ij}, t_k)$$

$$\forall s_{ij} \in S \ \& \ s_{ij} \rightarrow t_k \in \bar{a}$$

We propose an algorithm of order $O((V + A)Nlog(N) + K)$ to compute the K-best alignment configurations. First, the local scores of each verb and its dependents are computed for each word in the target sentence and stored in a local beam denoted by b_{ij}. The local beams corresponding to all the verbs and dependents are then sorted. This operation has the complexity $(V + A)\ N\ log(N)$.

The goal now is to pick the K-best configurations of alignment links. A single slot in the local beam corresponds to one alignment link. We define a boundary which partitions each local beam into two sets of slots. The slots above the boundary represent the slots which have been explored by the algorithm while slots below the boundary have still to be explored. The figure 3. shows the boundary which cuts across the local beams.

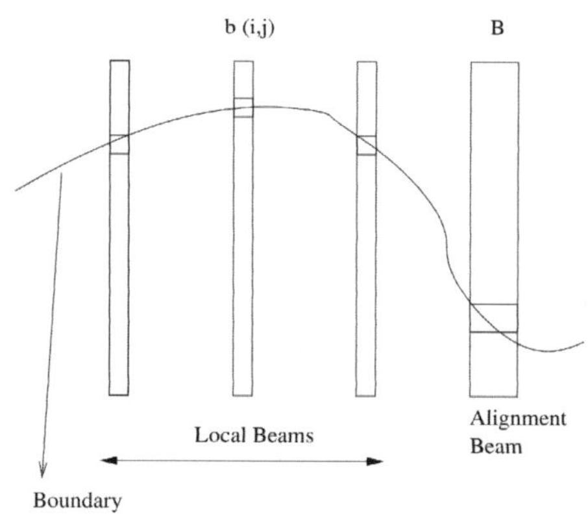

Figure 3: Boundary

We keep on modifying the boundary untill all the K slots in the Alignment Beam are filled with the K-best configurations. At the beginning of the algorithm, the boundary is a straight line passing through the top of all the local beams. The top slot of the alignment beam at the beginning represents the combination of alignment links with the best local scores.

The next slot $b_{ij}[p]$ (from the set of unexplored slots) to be included in the boundary is the slot which has the least difference in score from the score of the slot at the top of its local beam. That is, we pick the slot $b_{ij}[p]$ such that $score(b_{ij}[p]) - score(b_{ij}[1])$ is the least among all the unexplored slots (or alignment links). Trivially, $b_{ij}[p-1]$ was already a part of the boundary.

When the slot $b_{ij}[p]$ is included in the boundary, various configurations, which now contain $b_{ij}[p]$, are added to the alignment beam. The new configurations are the same as the ones which previously contained $b_{ij}[p-1]$ but with the replacement of $b_{ij}[p-1]$ by $b_{ij}[p]$. The above procedure ensures that the the alignment configurations are K-best and are sorted according to the scores obtained using local features.

4.2 Re-order the beam

We now use global features to re-order the beam. The global features look at the properties of the entire alignment configuration instead of alignment links locally.

The global score is defined as the dot product of the weight vector and the global feature vector.

$$score_G(\bar{a}) = W.f_G(\bar{a})$$

The overall score is calculated by adding the local score and the global score.

$$score(\bar{a}) = score_{La}(\bar{a}) + score_G(\bar{a})$$

The beam is now sorted based on the overall scores of each alignment. The alignment configuration at the top of the beam is the best possible alignment between source sentence and the target sentence.

4.3 Post-processing

The first two steps in our alignment algorithm compute alignments such that one verb or dependent in the source language side is aligned with only one word in the target side. But, in the case of compound verbs in Hindi, the verb in English is aligned to all the words which represent the compound verb in Hindi. For example, in Figure 3, the verb "lost" is aligned to both 'khoo' and 'dii'.

Our alignment algorithm would have aligned "lost" only to 'khoo'. Hence, we look at the window of words after the word which is aligned to

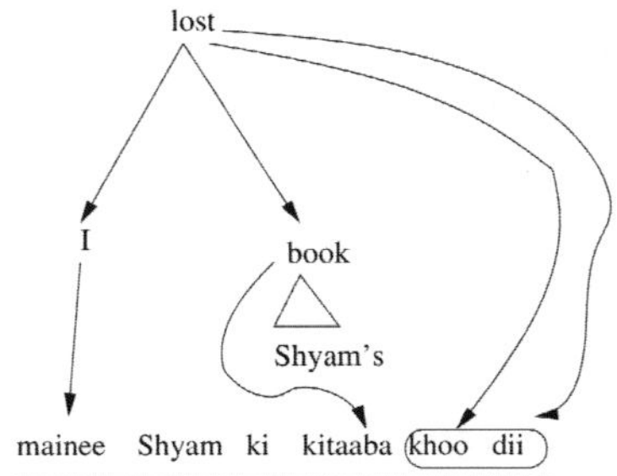

Figure 4: Case of compound verb in Hindi

the source verb and check if any of them is a verb which has not been aligned with any word in the source sentence. If this condition is satisfied, we align the source verb to these words too.

5 Parameters

As the number of training examples (294 sentences) is small, we choose to use very representative features. Some of the features which we used in this experiment are as follows,

5.1 Local features (F_L)

The local features which we consider are mainly co-occurence features. These features estimate the likelihood of a source word aligning to a target word based on the co-occurence information obtained from a large sentence aligned corpora[1].

1. **DiceWords**: Dice Coefficient of the source word and the target word

$$DCoeff(s_{ij}, t_k) = \frac{2 * Count(s_{ij}, t_k)}{Count(s_{ij}) + Count(t_k)}$$

   where $Count(s_{ij}, t_k)$ is the number of times the word t_k was present in the translation of sentences containing the word s_{ij} in the parallel corpus.

2. **DiceRoots**: Dice Coefficient of the lemmatized forms of the source and target words. It is important to consider this feature because the English-Hindi parallel corpus is not large and co-occurence information can be learnt effectively only after we lemmatize the words.

3. **Dict**: Whether there exists a dictionary entry from the source word s_{ij} to the target word

[1] 50K sentence pairs originally collected as part of TIDES MT project and later refined at IIIT-Hyderabad, India.

t_k. For English-Hindi, we used a dictionary available at IIIT - Hyderabad, India.

4. **Null**: Whether the source word s_{ij} is aligned to nothing in the target language.

5.2 Global features

The following are the four global features which we have considered,

- **AvgDist**: The average distance between the words in the target language sentence which are aligned to the verbs in the source language sentence . AvgDist is then normalized by dividing itself by the number of words in the target language sentence. If the average distance is small, it means that the verbs in the source language sentence are aligned with words in the target language sentence which are located at relatively close distances, relative to the length of the target language sentence.

  This feature expresses the distribution of predicates in the target language.

- **Overlap**: This feature stores the count of pairs of verbs in the source language sentence which align with the same word in the target language sentence. Overlap is normalized by dividing itself by the total pairs of verbs.

  This feature is used to discourage overlaps among the words which are alignments of verbs in the source language sentence.

- **MergePos**: This feature can be considered as a compositionality based feature. The part of speech tag of a dependent is essential to determine the likelihood of the dependent to align with the same word in the target language sentence as the word to which its verb is aligned.

  This binary feature is active when the alignment links of a dependent and its verb merge. For example, in Figure 5., the feature 'merge_RP' will be active (that is, merge_RP = 1).

- **MergeMI**: This is a compositionality based feature which associates point-wise mutual information (apart from the POS information) with the cases where the dependents which have the same alignment in the target language as their verbs. This features which notes the the compositionality value (represented by point-wise mutual information in our experiments) is active if the alignment links of dependent and its verb merge.

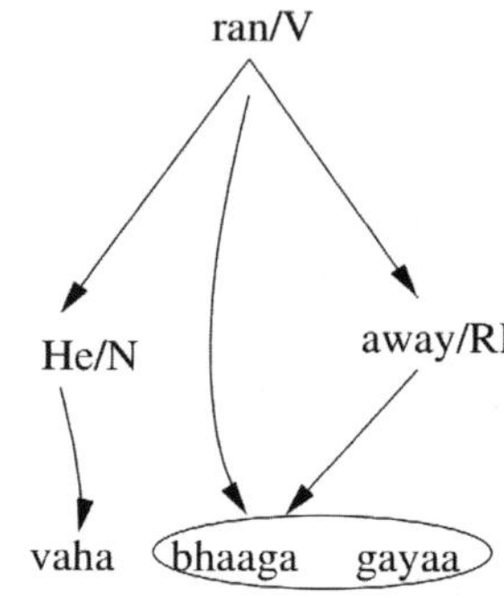

Figure 5: Example of MergePos feature

The mutual information (MI) is classified into three groups depending on its absolute value. If the absolute value of mutual information rounded to nearest integer is in the range 0-2, it is considered LOW. If the value is in the range 3-5, it is considered MEDIUM and if it is above 5, it is considered HIGH.

The feature "merge_RP_HIGH" is active in the example shown in figure 6.

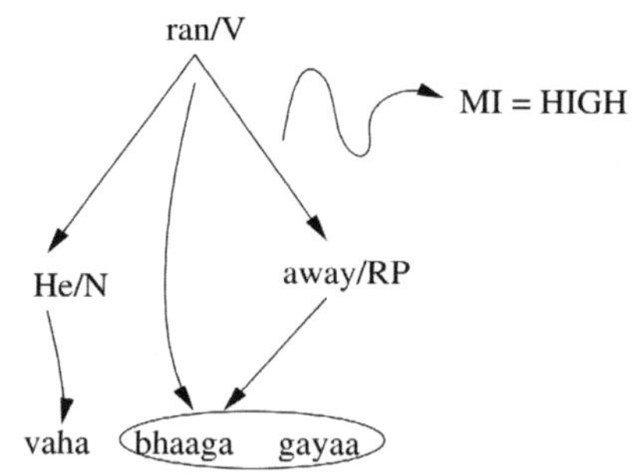

Figure 6: Example of MergeMI feature

6 Online large margin training

For parameter optimization, we have used an online large margin algorithm called MIRA (McDonald et al., 2005) (Crammer and Singer, 2003). We describe the training algorithm that we used very briefly. Our training set is a set of English-Hindi word aligned parallel corpus. We get the verb based expressions in English by running a dependency parser (Shen, 2006). Let the number of sentence pairs in the training data be m. We have

$\{S_q, T_q, \hat{a}_q\}$ for training where $q <= m$ is the index number of the sentence pair $\{S_q, T_q\}$ in the training set and $\hat{a}_q$ is the gold alignment for the pair $\{S_q, T_q\}$. Let W be the weight vector which has to be learnt, W_i be the weight vector after the end of ith update. To avoid over-fitting, W is obtained by averaging over all the weight vectors W_i.

A generic large margin algorithm is defined follows for the training instances $\{S_q, T_q, \hat{a}_q\}$,

1. Initialize W_0, W, i
2. for p:1 to NIterations
3. for q:1 to m
4. Get K-Best predictions $\alpha_q = \{a_1, a_2 ... a_k\}$ for the training example $(S_q, T_q, \hat{a_q})$ using the current model W^i and applying step 1 and 2 of section 4. Compute W^{i+1} by updating W^i based on $(S_q, T_q, \hat{a}_q, \alpha_q)$.
5. i = i + 1
6. $W = W + W^{i+1}$
7. $W = \frac{W}{NIterations * m}$

The goal of MIRA is to minimize the change in W^i such that the score of the gold alignment $\hat{a}$ exceeds the score of each of the predictions in α by a margin which is equal to the number of mistakes in the predictions when compared to gold alignment. While computing the number of mistakes, the mistakes due to the mis-alignment of head verb could be given greater weight, thus prompting the optimization algorithm to give greater importance to verb related mistakes and thereby improving overall performance.

Step 4 in the algorithm mentioned above can be substituted by the following optimization problem,

$$\begin{aligned}&\text{minimize } \|(W^{i+1} - W^i)\|\\ &\text{s.t. } \forall k,\ score(\hat{a}_q, S_q, T_q) - score(a_{q,k}, S_q, T_q)\\ &\qquad >= Mistakes(a_k, \hat{a}_q, S_q, T_q)\end{aligned}$$

The above optimization problem is converted to the Dual form using one Lagrangian multiplier for each constraint. In the Dual form, the Lagrangian multipliers are solved using Hildreth's algorithm. Here, prediction of α is similar to the prediction of $K - best$ classes in a multi-class classification problem. Ideally, we need to consider all the possible classes and assign margin constraints based on every class. But, here the number of such classes is exponential and thus we restrict ourselves to the $K - best$ classes.

7 Results on word-alignment task

7.1 Dataset

We have divided the 400 word aligned sentence pairs into a training set consisting of 294 sentence pairs and a test set consisting of 106 sentence pairs. The source sentences are all dependency parsed (Shen, 2006) and only the verb and its dependents are considered for both training and testing our algorithm. Our training algorithm requires that the each of the source words is aligned to only one or zero target words. For this, we use simple heuristics to convert the training data to the appropriate format. For the words aligned to a source verb, the first verb is chosen as the gold alignment. For the words aligned to any dependent which is not a verb, the last content word is chosen as the alignment link. For test data, we do not make any modifications and the final output from our alignment algorithm is compared with the original test data.

7.2 Experiments with Giza

We evaluated our discriminative approach by comparing it with the state-of-art Giza++ alignments (Och and Ney, 2003). The metric that we have used to do the comparison is the Alignment Error Rate (AER). The results shown below also contain Precision, Recall and F-measure.

Giza was trained using an English-Hindi aligned corpus of 50000 sentence pairs. In Table 1., we report the results of the GIZA++ alignments run from both the directions (English to Hindi and Hindi to English). We also show the results of the intersected model. See Table 1. for the results of the GIZA++ alignments.

	Prec.	Recall	F-meas.		AER
Eng → Hin	0.45	0.38	0.41		0.5874
Hin → Eng	0.46	0.27	0.34		0.6584
Intersected	0.82	0.19	0.31		0.6892

Table 1: Results of GIZA++ - Original dataset

We then lemmatize the words in both the source and target sides of the parallel corpora and then run Giza++ again. As the English-Hindi dataset of 50000 sentence pairs is relatively small, we expect lemmatizing to improve the results. Table 2. shows the results. As we hoped, the results after lemmatizing the word forms are better than those without.

	Prec.	Recall	F-meas.		AER
Eng → Hin	0.52	0.40	0.45		0.5518
Hin → Eng	0.53	0.30	0.38		0.6185
Intersected	0.82	0.23	0.36		0.6446

Table 2: Results of GIZA++ - lemmatized set

7.3 Experiments with our model

We trained our model using the training set of 294 word aligned sentence pairs. For training the parameters, we used a beam size of 3 and number of iterations equal to 3. Table 3. shows the results when we used only the basic local features (DiceWords, DiceRoots, Dict and Null) to train and test our model.

	Prec.	Recall	F-meas.		AER
Local Feats.	0.47	0.38	0.42		0.5798

Table 3: Results using the basic features

When we add the the global features (AvgDist, Overlap), we obtain the AER shown in Table 4.

	Prec.	Recall	F-meas.		AER
+ AvgD., Ove.	0.49	0.39	0.43		0.5689

Table 4: Results using the features - AvgDist, Overlap

Now, we add the transition probabilities obtained from the experiments with Giza++ as features in our model. Table 5. contains the results.

The compositionality related features are now added to our discriminative model to see if there is any improvement in performance. Table 6. shows the results by adding one feature at a time.

We observe that there is an improvement in the AER by using the compositionality based features, thus showing that compositionality based features aid in the word-alignment task in a significant way (AER = 0.5045).

	Prec.	Recall	F-meas.		AER
+ Giza++ prob.	0.54	0.44	0.49		0.5155

Table 5: Results using the Giza++ probabilities

	Prec.	Recall	F-meas.		AER
+ MergePos	0.54	0.45	0.49		0.5101
+ MergeMI	0.55	0.45	0.50		0.5045

Table 6: Results using the compositionality based features

8 Related work

Various measures have been proposed in the past to measure the compositionality of multi-word expressions of various types. Some of them are Frequency, Point-wise mutual information (Church and Hanks, 1989), Distributed frequency of object (Tapanainen et al., 1998), Distributed frequency of object using verb information (Venkatapathy and Joshi, 2005), Similarity of object in verb-object pair using the LSA model (Baldwin et al., 2003), (Venkatapathy and Joshi, 2005) and Lexical and Syntactic fixedness (Fazly and Stevenson, 2006). These features have largely been evaluated by the correlation of the compositionality value predicted by these measures with the gold standard value suggested by human judges. It has been shown that the correlation of these measures is higher than simple baseline measures suggesting that these measures represent compositionality quite well. But, the compositionality as such has not been used in any specific application yet.

In this paper, we have suggested a framework for using the compositionality of multi-word expressions for the word alignment task. State-of-art systems for doing word alignment use generative models like GIZA++ (Och and Ney, 2003; Brown et al., 1993). Discriminative models have been tried recently for word-alignment (Taskar et al., 2005; Moore, 2005) as these models give the ability to harness variety of complex features which cannot be provided in the generative models. In our work, we have used the compositionality of multi-word expressions to predict how they align with the words in the target language sentence.

For parameter optimization for the word-alignment task, Taskar, Simon and Klein (Taskar et al., 2005) used a large margin approach by factoring the structure level constraints to constraints at the level of an alignment link. We cannot do such a factorization because the scores of alignment links in our case are not computed in a completely isolated manner. We use an online large margin approach called MIRA (McDonald et al.,

2005; Crammer and Singer, 2003) which fits well with our framework. MIRA has previously been used by McDonald, Pereira, Ribarov and Hajic (McDonald et al., 2005) for learning the parameter values in the task of dependency parsing.

It should be noted that previous word-alignment experiments such as Taskar, Simon and Klein (Taskar et al., 2005) have been done with very large datasets and there is little word-order variation in the languages involved. Our dataset is small at present and there is substantial word order variation between the source and target languages.

9 Conclusion and future work

In this paper, we have proposed a discriminative approach for using the compositionality information about verb-based multi-word expressions for the word-alignment task. For training our model, use used an online large margin algorithm (McDonald et al., 2005). For predicting the alignment given a model, we proposed a K-Best beam search algorithm to make our prediction algorithm computationally feasible.

We have investigated the usefulness of simple features such as point-wise mutual information for the word-alignment task in English-Hindi bilingual corpus. We have show that by adding the compositionality based features to our model, we obtain an decrease in AER from 0.5155 to 0.5045. Our overall results are better than those obtained using the GIZA++ models (Och and Ney, 2003).

In future, we will experiment with more advanced compositionality based features. But, this would require a larger dataset for training and we are working towards buidling such a large dataset. Also, we would like to conduct similar experiments on other language pairs (e.g. English-French) and compare the results with the state-of-art results reported for those languages.

References

Timothy Baldwin, Colin Bannard, Takaaki Tanaka, and Dominic Widdows. 2003. An empirical model of multiword expression decomposability. In Diana McCarthy Francis Bond, Anna Korhonen and Aline Villavicencio, editors, *Proceedings of the ACL 2003 Workshop on Multiword Expressions: Analysis, Acquisition and Treatment*, pages 89–96.

P. Brown, S. A. Pietra, V. J. Della, Pietra, and R. L. Mercer. 1993. The mathmatics of stastistical machine translation. In *Computational Linguistics*.

Kenneth Church and Patrick Hanks. 1989. Word association norms, mutual information, and lexicography. In *Proceedings of the 27th. Annual Meeting of the Association for Computational Linguistics, 1990.*

Koby Crammer and Yoram Singer. 2003. Ultraconservative online algorithms for multiclass problems. In *Journal of Machine Learning Research.*

Afsaneh Fazly and Suzanne Stevenson. 2006. Automatically constructing a lexicon of verb phrase idiomatic combinations. In *Proceedings of European Chapter of Association of Computational Linguistics*. Trento, Italy, April.

Ryan McDonald, Fernando Pereira, Kiril Ribarov, and Jan Hajic. 2005. Non-projective dependency parsing using spanning tree algorithms. In *Proceedings of Human Language Technology Conference and Conference on Empirical Methods in Natural Language Processing*, pages 523–530, Vancouver, British Columbia, Canada, October. Association of Computational Linguistics.

Robert C. Moore. 2005. A discriminative framework for bilingual word alignment. In *Proceedings of Human Language Technology Conference and Conference on Empirical Methods in Natural Language Processing*, pages 81–88, Vancouver, British Columbia, Canada, October. Association of Computational Linguistics.

F. Och and H. Ney. 2003. A systematic comparisoin of various statistical alignment models. In *Computational Linguistics.*

Ivan A. Sag, Timothy Baldwin, Francis Bond, Ann Copestake, and Dan Flickinger. 2002. Multi-word expressions: a pain in the neck for nlp. In *Proceedings of CICLing , 2002.*

Libin Shen. 2006. *Statistical LTAG Parsing*. Ph.D. thesis.

Pasi Tapanainen, Jussi Piitulaine, and Timo Jarvinen. 1998. Idiomatic object usage and support verbs. In *36th Annual Meeting of the Association for Computational Linguistics.*

Ben Taskar, Locoste-Julien Simon, and Klein Dan. 2005. A discriminative machine learning approach to word alignment. In *Proceedings of Human Language Technology Conference and Conference on Empirical Methods in Natural Language Processing*, pages 73–80, Vancouver, British Columbia, Canada, October. Association of Computational Linguistics.

Sriram Venkatapathy and Aravind Joshi. 2005. Measuring the relative compositionality of verb-noun (v-n) collocations by integrating features. In *Proceedings of Human Language Technology Conference and Conference on Empirical Methods in Natural Language Processing*, pages 899–906. Association of Computational Linguistics, Vancouver, British Columbia, Canada, October.

Detecting Complex Predicates in Hindi using POS Projection across Parallel Corpora

Amitabha Mukerjee, Ankit Soni, and
Dept. of Computer Science and Engg
Indian Institute of Technology Kanpur
Kanpur -208016, India
amit@iitk.ac.in,
ankit@iitk.ac.in

Achla M Raina
Dept. of Humanities and Social Sciences
Indian Institute of Technology Kanpur
Kanpur -208016, India
achla@iitk.ac.in

Abstract

Complex Predicates or CPs are multi-word complexes functioning as single verbal units. CPs are particularly pervasive in Hindi and other Indo-Aryan languages, but an usage account driven by corpus-based identification of these constructs has not been possible since single-language systems based on rules and statistical approaches require reliable tools (POS taggers, parsers, etc.) that are unavailable for Hindi. This paper highlights the development of first such database based on the simple idea of projecting POS tags across an English-Hindi parallel corpus. The CP types considered include adjective-verb (AV), noun-verb (NV), adverb-verb (Adv-V), and verb-verb (VV) composites. CPs are hypothesized where a verb in English is projected onto a multi-word sequence in Hindi. While this process misses some CPs, those that are detected appear to be more reliable (83% precision, 46% recall). The resulting database lists usage instances of 1439 CPs in 4400 sentences.

1 Introduction

A "pain in the neck" (Sag et al., 2002) for NLP in languages of the Indo-Aryan family (e.g. Hindi-Urdu, Bangla and Kashmiri) is the fact that most verbs (nearly half of all instances in Hindi) occur as *complex predicates* - multi-word complexes which function as a single verbal unit in terms of argument and event structure (Hook, 1993; Butt and Geuder, 2003; Raina and Mukerjee, 2005). Moreover, most of these languages being resource-poor, even a proper corpus-based characterization of such CPs has remained an elusive goal.

In this paper we construct the first corpus-based lexicon of CPs in Hindi based on projecting POS tags across parallel English-Hindi corpora. While such approaches sometimes leave out some CPs, the ones that are identified are seen to be quite robust. As a result, this appears to be a good first approach for identifying the majority of CPs along with usage data. Moreover, since the language specific input in the procedure is minimal, it can be easily extended to other languages with similar multi word expressions.

2 Complex Predicates

CPs are characterized by a predicate or host - typically a noun (N), adjective (A), verb (V), or adverb (Adv) - followed by a *light verb* (LV), a grammaticalized version of a main verb, which contributes little telic significance to the composite predicate. As an example, the English verb "describe" may be rendered in Hindi as the Noun-Verb complex 'वर्णन + कर', *varNan kar*, "description + do". Analysis based on a non-CP lexicon might assign the verbal head as *kar* (do), whereas functional aspects such as the argument structure are determined by the noun host *varNan* "description". An example of a V-V CP may

Proceedings of the Workshop on Multiword Expressions: Identifying and Exploiting Underlying Properties, pages 28–35,
Sydney, July 2006. ©2006 Association for Computational Linguistics

be 'कर + दे', kar *de* "do+give", where the light verb *de* "give" imposes a completive aspect on the action kar "do".

Identifying such constructs is a significant hurdle for NLP tasks ranging from phrasal parsing (Ray et al., 2003, Shrivastava et al., 2005), translation (where each complex may be treated as a lexical unit in the target language), predicate-argument analysis, to semantic delineation. In addition to the computational aspects, a mere listing of all CPs occurring in the corpus would provide an important resource for tasks such as constructing WordNets (Narayan et al.,2002) and linguistic analysis of CPs (Butt and Geuder, 2003).

Rule-based approaches to identifying CPs are not very effective since there do not seem to be any clear set of rules that can be used to distinguish CPs from non-CP constructs (contrast, for example, the composite CP 'अनुमति दे' *anumati de* "permission+give" with the non-composite N-V structure 'किताब दे' *kitaab de* "give the book"). Even where such rules do exist, they depend on semantic properties such as the fact that book is a physical object which can be given in the physical sense (Raina and Mukerjee, 2005). However, in the translated form, the former may show up as a verb, whereas the latter invariably will be a N+V, so the tag projection would rule out the latter as a CP.

Here we adopt a parallel corpus-based approach to creating a database of complex predicates in Hindi. The procedure can potentially be duplicated to most Indo-Aryan languages. The motivation is that a CP may be translated as a direct verb in other languages, and POS Projection across Parallel Corpora then project a tag of Verb for this expression in the source language. Additional linguistic constraints are used to determine if the multi-word cluster qualifies as a CP. These include a check list of LVs that can occur with A, N, V and Adv constituents of a multi word predicate.

Let us consider some examples from the CP lexicon constructed from the EMILLE parallel corpus (McEnery et al., 2000) of 200,000 words, collected from leaflets prepared by the UK government for immigrants. Examples of these different complexes may be:

(1) N+V: वर्णन + कर *varNan kar*
"description + do":

पैकेज या प्रस्तुत इश्तेहार में जैसे
paikej yaa prastut ishtehaar mein jaise
package or present advertisement in as

वर्णन किया गया हो, ठीक वैसा
varNan kiyaa gayaa ho Thlk vaisaa
description do-past go-past be-pres exact same

ही होगा
hii hogaa
emph be-fut

"It will be exactly as described on the package or the display advertisement."

(2) A+V: उपलब्ध है *upalabdh hai*
"available+ be":

सहायता समीप ही उपलब्ध है।
Sahaytaa samiip hii upalabdh hai
Help near emph available be-pres

"Help is available nearby."

(3) V+V : सोच ले *soch le* "think+take":

पहले हर पहलू के बारे में अच्छी तरह
Pahle har pehluu ke baare-mein achchhi tarah
First every aspect-poss about good way

सोच लीजिए।
soch liijiye
think take-imp-hon

"Think it through first."

(4) Adv+V *vaapas paa* "return+obtain"

आप सामान बदलने में अपने पूरे पैसे
Aap saamaan badalne mein apne puure paise
You goods exchange-nom in your all money

वापस पाने का अधिकार खो देते हैं।
vaapas paane kaa adhikar kho dete hai
return obtain-nom of right lose give be-pres

"You loose your right to get your full money back in exchanging the goods. "

Of the four classes cited above, the NV and AV classes are the most productive. The AdvV class is highly restricted, confined to a few adverbs. The VV class is highly selective for its constituents, apparently driven by semantic considerations.

Identifying CPs in text is crucial to processing since it serves as a clausal head, and other elements in the phrase are licensed by the complex as a whole and not by the verbal head. The semantic import of the host-verb complex varies along a composability continuum, at one end of which we have purely idiomatic CPs, while at the other end, the CPs may be recoverable from its constituents. For example, 'व्यवहार+कर', vyavhaar *kar*, "behave+do" has a sense of "use,treat" in English, reflecting clearly an idiomatic usage.

Detecting CPs is made difficult by the differing degrees of productivity for different classes of open-class host, which reflects the applicability of unrestricted rules. Also, verbs participating in CPs are very selective; e.g. in NV and AV CPs the verb is typically restricted to *ho, kar* and the like, whereas in VV constructs ho reflects auxiliary usage, but a different set of verbs appear. The open class word (host) tends to be uninflected, and only the light verb (LV) carries tense, agreement and aspect markers. Even the host V participating in a VV CP is always uninflected. As an instance of the difficulty in detecting CPs, consider the so called permissive CP (Hook, 1993; Butt and Geuder, 2003), as in the *karne+de* "do-nom +give" example here, where the host verb appears to be inflected:

(5) Raam ne sitaa ko kaam karne diyaa
Ram-erg sita-acc work do-nom give-past
"Ram let Sita do the work"

However, this does not actually reflect CP usage, and is better parsed as:

(6) $[_S$ $[_{NP}$ raam ne] $[_{VP}$ $[_{NP}$ sitaa ko] $[_{VP}$ kaam karne] $[_V$ diyaa] $_{VP}]$ $_S]$

Another challenge for CP identification is that the constituents may be separated – sometimes quite widely.

3 CPs from Parallel Projection

Identifying MWEs from corpora is clearly an area of increasing research emphasis. For resource-rich languages, one may use a parse tree and look for mutual information statistics in head-complement collocations, and also compare it with other "similar" collocations to determine if something is unusual about a given construct (Lin, 1999). As of now however, even POS-tagging remains a challenge for languages such as Hindi, thereby making it necessary to seek alternate methods.

Parallel corpus based approaches to inducing monolingual part-of-speech taggers, base noun-phrase bracketers, named-entity taggers and morphological analyzers for French, Chinese and other languages have shown quite promising results (Yarowsky et al., 2001). These approaches use minimal linguistic input and have been increasingly effective with the growth in the availability of large parallel corpuses. The algorithm essentially attempts to word-align the target language sentences with the source language sentences and then use a probabilistic model try to project the linguistic information from the source language. Since these are statistical algorithms, the accuracy of results depends on the size of the corpus used.

In our approach, we first use a similar approach to word-align an English-Hindi parallel corpus. The English sentences are tagged and the tags are projected to Hindi sentences. We observe that words which are tagged as verbs by projection and have POS tag as N, A, Adv or V in the Hindi lexicon, and are followed by an LV, are usually CPs.

Clearly the CP detection is limited to those instances where a CP in the target language is translated as a single verb in English. For example, a phrase such as जवाब दे, *jawaab de,* "answer give", may be rendered in English either as the verb "answer" or as the English CP "give answer". In the latter case (an example appearing quite frequently in this corpus), the correct POS projection would label jawaab as [N answer], thus failing to detect the CP. While this may not be significant in certain tasks (e.g. translation), it may be relevant in others (e.g. semantic processing).

Furthermore, the POS tagging process is inherently biased towards projecting tags for frequently encountered constituents first, and this may lead to some constituents in certain CPs being flagged with their normal POS tags, resulting in missed CPs. However, this does not result in false positives, since non-CP constructs often fail on other criteria (e.g. list of LVs).

For reasons discussed above, many CPs are not identifiable through parallel corpus methods. Some examples include 'अधिकार होते', 'पैदा करने', 'हानि होती'. Our database is therefore correspondingly thin for these types of CPs.

With VV CPs, it is difficult to distinguish between CPs and other related structures such as the passive construct or serial verbs. These are illustrated below.

(7) Passive

ऐसा	भी	हो	सकता	है	कि	क्रेडिट	नोट
Aisa	*bhii*	*ho*	*saktaa*	*hai*	*ki*	*credit*	*note*
It	emph	be	can	aux	that	credit	note

सिर्फ	कुछ	ही	दिनों	तक	काम	में
siraf	*kuch*	*hii*	*dino*	*tak*	*kaam*	*me*
only	few	emph	days	for	use	in

लाया	जा	सकता	हो।
laaya	*jaa*	*sakta*	*ho*
bring	go	can	be

"It is quite possible that the credit note can be put to use only for a few days."

(8) Serial verb

वह	लडका	मुझे	अपनी	किताब	दे	गया।
voh	*laDkaa*	*mujhe*	*apni*	*kitaab*	*de*	*gayaa*
That	boy	me	own	book	give	go-past

"That boy gave me his book and went away."

It appears that passive can be reliably ruled out using the root verb criterion for VVs, since the main verb in passive is always in an inflected form. No comparable formal criterion exists for the serial verb, where also the POS tagger will identify both constituents as verbs. However, these verbs are relatively rare compared to CPs.

4 Hindi-English POS Projection

4.1 Data Resources and Preprocessing

We used the EMILLE[1] corpus Hindi-English parallel corpus, with approximately 200,000 words in non-sentenced aligned translations in Unicode 16 format (McEnery et al., 2000). The texts consist of different types of information leaflets originally in English, along with translations in Hindi, Bangla, Gujarati and a number of South Asian languages. Closer analysis of the corpus reveals that the corpus is not completely sentence aligned and also that the translations are not very correct in many cases. Hindi versions of the manuals tend to be more verbose than their English translations.

For the word alignment algorithm we needed a sentence aligned corpus but due to the small size of the parallel corpus, the standard sentence alignment systems did not give very high accuracy levels. Therefore, the whole data was manually sentence aligned to produce a sentence aligned parallel corpus of about nine thousand sentences and 140 thousand words which is used in this work.

4.2 Word alignment

We have used IBM models proposed by Brown (Brown et al., 1993) for word aligning the parallel corpus. The IBM models have been widely used in statistical machine translation. Given a Hindi sentence h, we seek the English sentence e that maximizes P(e | h); the "most likely" translation.

Now $P(e \mid h) = P(e) * P(h \mid e) / P(h)$
argmax-e $P(e \mid h) =$ argmax-e $P(e) * P(h \mid e)$.

P (e) is modeled by the N-gram model .We are interested in P (h | e). We used the Giza++ tool kit (Och and Ney, 2000), based on the Expectation Maximization (EM) algorithm, to calculate these probability measures. At the end of this step, we have a word-to-word mapping between the English and Hindi sentences. A "NULL" is used in the English sentences to account for the unaligned Hindi words from the corresponding Hindi sentence.

[1] http://bowland-files.lancs.ac.uk/corplang/emille/

Figure 1. Example of projection of POS tags from English to Hindi. Here the phrase "shikaayat kar" is projected from the English "complain" and is tagged as V+V. Since shikaayat is a N in the Hindi lexicon, this phrase is identified as an CP of N+V type.

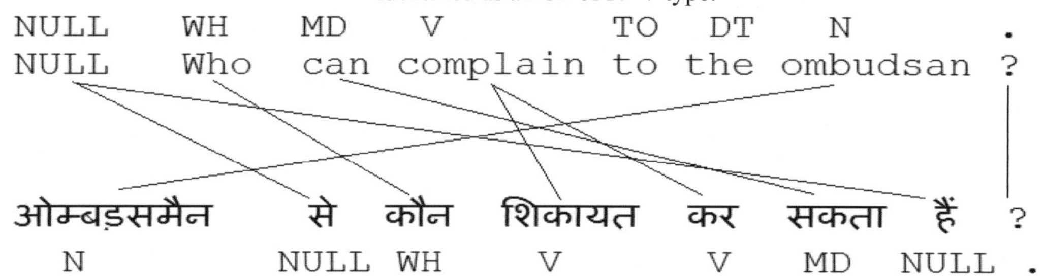

4.3 Tagging English Sentences

The English sentences are POS-tagged using the Brill Tagger (Brill, 1994), a rule based tagger which uses more or less the same tags as the Penn Treebank project (Marcus, 1994). Since for our purposes, we did not need a very detailed subcategorization of the tag set for Hindi, the English tag set was reduced by merging the subcategorization tags of a few categories. Thus all noun distinctions in the Pen Treebank tagset based on number, person etc were merged in our treatment of the Noun class. Similarly in the case of verbs, we merged distinctions based on tense, person, aspect and participles etc. Subclasses of adverbs and case forms of pronouns were also merged. Rest of the POS categories were retained. The "NULL" word in the English sentences, used for unaligned Hindi words in the parallel corpus, was given a "NULL" tag.

4.4 Projection of Tags to Hindi

The reduced English tags were projected to Hindi words based on the word alignments obtained earlier. A sample alignment and tagged projection is shown in Figure 1. As the figure shows, postpositional markers, which are relatively more frequent in Hindi are mapped to the "NULL" word in the English sentence.

Since the amount of training data is very small, the statistical word alignment algorithm is not adequate enough to align all words correctly. To overcome this weakness, we apply some filtering conditions to remove alignment errors, especially in smaller sentences. This filtering is based on two parameters: a) Fertility count (r_f), which is defined as the number of Hindi words an English word maps to, and b) Acceptance level (k), defined as the number of words acceptable in a sentence with fertility count greater than equal to r_f. These two parameters are selected to minimize errors in the groundtruth sample-set, and the resulting filtering heuristics used are presented in Table 1.

Table-1. Filtering Criteria

	Sentence Length	Fertility Count(r_f)	Acceptance Level(k)
1.	1-5	2	1
2.	5-10	3	2
3.	10-15	3	3
4.	15-20	4	3
5.	20-25	4	3
6.	25-35	4	3
7.	35+	4	3

4.5 Identification of CP's

After the filtering is done we observe that the CP's are usually translated as a direct verb in English. So if the projected tag of a Hindi word is Verb and the normal POS tag of the word in the Hindi dictionary is N, A, V or Adv and the word is followed by one of the members from the LV set, then we classify the multi word expression as N+V, A+V, V+V, or Adv+V CP respectively.

4.6 Fragments of the CP Lexicon

A sample fragment of the CP lexicon is shown in Figure-2. The whole corpus is available online[2]. Since we do not have a very comprehensive Hindi dictionary we are not able to classify many CP's that are identified in their respective class. On a test with 4400 sentences we identified a total of 1439 CPs

[2] The lexicon is available online at http://www.cse.iitk.ac.in/users/language/CP-database.htm

Figure 2. Example of the CP lexicon for “shikaayat kr”

N+V Complex Predicate शिकायत + कर

1. हालाँकि कुछ लोग शिकायत करते हैं , जिस हद तक उन्हें सफलता मिलती है वह अलग-अलग होती है ।
2. पर यह बात तब नहीं लागू होती है जब 'सामान स्वीकार करने' के बाद आप उसकी किसी गड़बड़ी की शिकायत करते हैं , या आपको वह सामान तोहफे के रूप में मिला हो ।
3. जब आप शिकायत करते हैं , तो हमेशा अपनी बातों को सही पता कर लीजिए और शांत रहिए ।
4. ओम्बड्समैन से कौन शिकायत कर सकता हैं ?
5. किस बारे में शिकायत कर सकता/सकती हूँ ?
6. इस लिये शिकायत करने से पूर्व सब से पहले सम्बन्धित व्यक्ति से बात करें।
7. उस संस्था के बारे में जिसके विरुद्ध आप शिकायत कर रहे हैं?
8. आप किस एन एच एस (NHS) संस्था या प्रैक्टीशनर के बारे में शिकायत कर रहे हैं?
9. अगर आपने दाम नहीं तय किए थे और जब बिल आता है , तो आपको लगता है कि आपसे अधिक दाम लिए गए हैं , तो शिकायत करने पर तुलना करने के लिए दूसरे व्यापारियों से कोटेशंज़ लीजिए ।
10. गारंटियाँ आपको अतिरिक्त अधिकार देती हैं जो शिकायत करने की ज़रूरत पड़ने पर काम आ सकतीं हैं ।

with the following distribution: N+V: 788, A+V: 107, Adv+V: 18 and V+V: 526.

4.7 Errors in CP identification

CP identification in the test data set involved certain ground truth decisions such as excluding verbal composites with regular auxiliary verb है, *hai* corresponding to the English finite verb ‘be’ and the progressive ‘रहा’ raha ‘-ing (progressive)’. CPs with idiomatic usage were included, and so were the CPs with a passive verb, although the latter were not counted in computational scores. The testing was done on a small set of about 120 groundtruth sentences in which the CP’s were carefully identified manually. We get a precision of about 82.5% and a recall of 40% with our CP finding algorithm. If the idiomatic CPs is not considered the recall goes upto 46%.

Several types of errors are observed in the corpus-derived results. A False Negative (missed CP) error arising due to the English complex predicate is shown in Figure 3. A number of False Positives arise due to inadequacy in the Hindi dictionary – the online dictionary of Hindi we used was missing many lexemes. A further problem is homography – e.g. the word *kii* (do-past) appears both as an possessive marker, as well as the past-tense form for the verb *kara* (do), occurring frequently (with jaa, go) in adjectival clause constructions. This has been mis-tagged in about one in ten instances (approx 0.2% cases), with hosts such as *shikaayat* (complaint), *baat* (talk), *dekhvaal* (looking-after), *madad* (help) etc. Similarly, the word *un* can appear as a noun (wool) or a pronoun (he). Furthermore, while considerable care was taken to manually sentence align the parallel corpus, a number of typos and other problems remain, some of them show up as false positives.

4.8 Discontinuous CP identification

In the results above, we have made no attempt to identify discontinuous CPs, i.e., instances where other phonological material intervenes between the constituents of a CP, As an example, consider

(9) जाँच हो, jaanch ho, “inspection-be”

अगर	कार	की	जाँच	पहले	ही हो
agar	*kaar*	*kii*	*jaanch*	*pahale*	*hii ho*
if	car	poss	inspection	earlier	emph happen

चुकी	है ,	तो	रिपोर्ट	माँगिए ।
chuki	*hai*	*to*	*report*	*mangiye*
comp.	be-present	then	report	ask-imp-hon

“If the car has already been inspected please ask to see the report.”

These separated multi-word expressions constitute some of the most difficult problems for any language – for example, one may compare these with English phrasal verbs like “give up”, which can sometimes occur in discontinuity. However, owing to the relatively free word order in Hindi, the discontinuous CPs in Hindi are separated by a variety of structures ranging from simple emphatic or focal particles and negation markers to clausal

Figure 3. Here the projection process fails to detect the CP "shikaayat karna" since the English translation is also CP "make complaint". Improvements in MWE detection in English can possibly help reduce such errors.

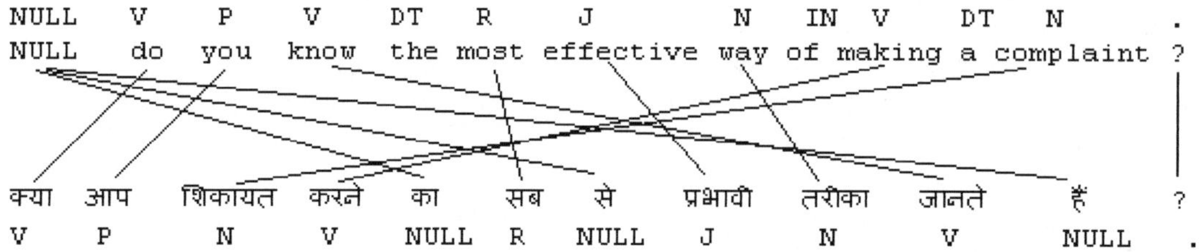

Figure 4. A verb in the source language, "inspected" projects to *jaanch* (inspection)+ *ho* (be) + *chukaa hai* (aux), although they are separated by the phrase *pahale-bhi* (already). Thus, using source and target languages together. the parallel projection method may have the potential for discovering discontinuous CPs as well.

constituents. How these structures are to be encoded in a computational lexicon is a complex matter that takes us beyond CP identification (Villavicencio et al. 2004). But while rule-based identification of such constructs is problematic, we feel that POS-tag projection holds considerable promise in this direction.

In the algorithm above we have only considered the target language (Hindi) tags after the parallel tagging is completed. If in addition, we also consider the source language tag and its radiation the CP probabilities may be redefined in a manner that helps capture some discontinuous CPs as well. Thus, if English "complain" radiates to *shikaayat* and *kara*, the inherent CP can be detected even in the presence of an intermediate phrase. An example from the POS-tagged data exhibiting discontinous CP detection is presented in Figure 4.

5 Conclusion

In this work we have presented a preliminary approach to a corpus-based lexicon of CPs in Hindi based on projecting POS tags across parallel English-Hindi corpora. Since the approach involves minimal linguistic analysis, it is easily extendable to other languages which exhibit similar CP constructs, provided the availability of a POS lexicon.

Clearly, a number of problems will remain with any such approach. The limitiations of the parallel POS tagging is that certain kinds of maps may never be found (as in parallel CPs in source and target languages). On the other hand, some of our accuracies, we feel, would improve considerably given a larger parallel corpus and more refined use of a Hindi lexicon.

In addition to the handling of discontinuous CPs hinted at above, another aspect that we would like to consider next is to tune some of the parameters of the parallel tagging algorithm, such as specifically tuning the distortion and fertility probabilities in situations (e.g. English verbs) that are likely to manifest CPs in Hindi.

We feel that beyond the usefulness of this initial approach, the database of CPs constructed in this work may in itself be an important linguistic resource for Hindi. Furthermore, the approach can possibly be used to detect MWEs that radiate to a single lexical structure in another language, e.g. phrasal verbs in English.

Acknowledgements We acknowledge a comment from an anonymous reviewer regarding discontinuous CPs which led us to investigate them (Figure 4 above). However, it was not possible to report this important exception for the entire database.

References

Eric Brill.1994. *Some advances in transformation-based part of speech tagging*, National Conference on Artificial Intelligence,p 722-727.

Peter F. Brown, Pietra, S. A. D., Pietra, V. J. D., & Mercer, R. L.. 1993. Computational Linguistics 19(2), 263-311.

Miriam Butt and Wilhelm Geuder. 2003. *Light Verbs in Urdu and Grammaticalization.*, Trends in Linguistics Studies and Monographs, Vol 143, p295-350.

Peter E. Hook. 1993. *Aspectogenesis and the Compound Verb in Indo-Aryan.* Complex Predicates in South Asian Languages.

Dekang Lin.1999. *Automatic Identification of Non-compositional Phrases*, Proceedings of the 37th Annual Meeting of the Association for Computational Linguistics, 317--324.

Mitchell P. Marcus, Beatrice Santorini and Mary Ann Marcinkiewicz. 1994. *Building a large annotated corpus of English: the Penn Treebank,* Computational Linguistics 19(2), 313–330.

A. M. McEnery, P. Baker, R. Gaizauskas, and H. Cunningham. 2000. *EMILLE: Building a Corpus of South Asian Languages*, Vivek, A Quarterly in Artiificial Intelligence, 13(3):p 23–32.

D Narayan, D Chakrabarty, P Pande and P Bhattacharyya. 2002. *Experiences in Building the Indo Wordnet: A Wordnet for Hindi* International Conference on Global WordNet

Franz Josef Och and Hermann Ney. 2000. *Improved statistical alignment models*, in ACL00 p 440–447.

Achla M. Raina and Amitabha Mukerjee. 2005. *Complex predicates in the generative lexicon*, Proceedings of GL'2005, Third International Workshop on Generative Approaches to the Lexicon, p210-221.

Pradipta Ranjan Ray, Harish V. Sudeshna Sarkar and Anupam Basu.. 2003. *Part of Speech Tagging and Local Word Grouping Techniques for Natural Language Parsing in Hindi.* In Proceedings of (ICON) 2003.

Ivan Sag, Timothy Baldwin, Francis Bond, Ann Copestake and Dan Flickinger. 2002. *Multiword expressions: A pain in the neck for NLP* ,Proceedings of the 3rd International Conference on Intelligent Text Processing and Computational Linguistics (CICLing-2002) ,p1-15.

Manish Shrivastava, Nitin Agrawal, Smriti Singh and Pushpak Bhattacharya. 2005. *Harnessing Morphological Analysis in POS Tagging Task*, In Proceedings ICON 2005.

Aline Villavicencio, Ann Copestake, Benjamin Waldron, and Fabre Lambeau. 2004. *The Lexical Encoding of MWEs* , Proceedings Second ACL Workshop on Multiword Expressions: Integrating Processing, p80-87.

David Yarowsky, G. Ngai, and R. Wicentowski. 2001. *Inducing multilingual pos taggers and np bracketers via robust projection across aligned corpora*, Proceedings of Human Language Technology Conference .p1 - 8.

Automated Multiword Expression Prediction for Grammar Engineering

Yi Zhang & **Valia Kordoni**
Dept. of Computational Linguistics
Saarland University
D-66041 Saarbrücken, Germany
{yzhang,kordoni}@coli.uni-sb.de

Aline Villavicencio & **Marco Idiart**
Institutes of Informatics & Physics
Federal University of Rio Grande do Sul
Av. Bento Gonçalves, 9500
Porto Alegre - RS, Brazil
avillavicencio@inf.ufrgs.br
idiart@if.ufrgs.br

Abstract

However large a hand-crafted wide-coverage grammar is, there are always going to be words and constructions that are not included in it and are going to cause parse failure. Due to their heterogeneous and flexible nature, Multiword Expressions (MWEs) provide an endless source of parse failures. As the number of such expressions in a speaker's lexicon is equiparable to the number of single word units (Jackendoff, 1997), one major challenge for robust natural language processing systems is to be able to deal with MWEs. In this paper we propose to semi-automatically detect MWE candidates in texts using some error mining techniques and validating them using a combination of the World Wide Web as a corpus and some statistical measures. For the remaining candidates possible lexico-syntactic types are predicted, and they are subsequently added to the grammar as new lexical entries. This approach provides a significant increase in the coverage of these expressions.

1 Introduction

Hand-crafted large-scale grammars like the English Resource Grammar (Flickinger, 2000), the Pargram grammars (Butt et al., 1999) and the Dutch Alpino Grammar (Bouma et al., 2001) are extremely valuable resources that have been used in many NLP applications. However, due to the open-ended and dynamic nature of languages, and the difficulties of grammar engineering, such grammars are likely to contain errors and be incomplete. An error can be roughly classified as *under-generating* (if it prevents a grammatical sentence to be generated/parsed) or *over-generating* (if it allows an ungrammatical sentence to be generated/parsed). In the context of wide-coverage parsing, we focus on the *under-generating* errors which normally lead to parsing failure.

Traditionally, the errors of the grammar are to be detected manually by the grammar developers. This is usually done by running the grammar over a carefully designed test suite and inspecting the outputs. This procedure becomes less reliable as the grammar gets larger, and is especially difficult when the grammar is developed in a distributed manner. Baldwin et al. (2004), among many others, for instance, have investigated the main causes of parse failure, parsing a random sample of 20,000 strings from the written component of the British National Corpus (henceforward BNC) using the English Resource Grammar (Flickinger, 2000), a broad-coverage precision HPSG grammar for English. They have found that the large majority of failures are caused by missing lexical entries, with 40% of the cases, and missing constructions, with 39%.

To this effect, as mentioned above, in recent years, some approaches have been developed in order to (semi)automatically detect and/or repair the errors in linguistic grammars. van Noord (2004), for instance, takes a statistical approach towards semi-automated error detection using the parsability metric for word sequences. He reports on a simple yet practical way of identifying grammar errors. The method is particularly useful for discovering systematic problems in a large grammar with reasonable coverage. The idea behind it is that each (under-generating) error in the gram-

Proceedings of the Workshop on Multiword Expressions: Identifying and Exploiting Underlying Properties, pages 36–44,
Sydney, July 2006.

mar leads to the parsing failure of some specific grammatical sentences. By running the grammar over a large corpus, the corpus can be split into two subsets: the set of sentences covered by the grammar and the set of sentences that failed to parse. The errors can be identified by comparing the *statistical difference* between these two sets of sentences. By *statistical difference*, any kind of uneven distribution of linguistic phenomena is meant. In the case of van Noord (2004), the word sequences are used, mainly because the cost to compute and count the word sequences is minimum. The parsability of a sequence $w_i \dots w_j$ is defined as:

$$R(w_i \dots w_j) = \frac{C(w_i \dots w_j, OK)}{C(w_i \dots w_j)} \quad (1)$$

where $C(w_i \dots w_j)$ is the number of sentences in which the sequence $w_i \dots w_j$ occurs, and $C(w_i \dots w_j, OK)$ is the number of sentences with a successful parse which contain the sequence. A frequency cut is used to eliminate the infrequent sequences. With suffix arrays and perfect hashing automata, the parsability of all word sequences (with arbitrary length) can be computed efficiently. The word sequences are then sorted according to their parsabilities. Those sequences with the lowest parsabilities are taken as direct indication of grammar errors.

Among them, one common error, and subsequently very common cause of parse failure is due to Multiword Expressions (MWEs), like phrasal verbs (*break down*), collocations (*bread and butter*), compound nouns (*coffee machine*), determiner-less PPs (*in hospital*), as well as so-called "frozen expressions" (*by and large*), as discussed by both Baldwin et al. (2004) and van Noord (2004). Indicatively, in the experiments reported in Baldwin et al. (2004), for instance, from all the errors due to missing lexical entries, one fifth were due to missing MWEs (8% of total errors). If an MWE is syntactically marked, the standard grammatical rules and lexical entries cannot generate the string, as for instance in the case of a phrasal verb like *take off*, even if the individual words that make up the MWE are contained in the lexicon.

In this paper we investigate semi-automatic methods for error mining and detection of missing lexical entries, following van Noord (2004), with the subsequent handling of the MWEs among them. The output of the error mining phase proposes a set of n-grams, which also contain MWEs. Therefore, the task is to distinguish the MWEs from the other cases. To do this, first we propose to use the World Wide Web as a very large corpus from which we collect evidence that enables us to rule out noisy cases (due to spelling errors, for instance), following Grefenstette (1999), Keller et al. (2002), Kilgarriff and Grefenstette (2003) and Villavicencio (2005). The candidates that are kept can be semi-automatically included in the grammar, by employing a lexical type predictor, whose output we use in order to add lexical entries to the lexicon, with a possible manual check by a grammar writer. This procedure significantly speeds up the process of grammar development, relieving the grammar developer of some of the burden by automatically detecting parse failures and providing semi-automatic means for handling them.

The paper starts with a discussion of MWEs and of some of the characteristics that make them so challenging for NLP, in section 2. This is followed by a more detailed discussion of the technique employed for error detection, in section 3. The approach used for distinguishing noisy sequences from MWE-related constructions using the World Wide Web is then presented. How this information is used for extending the grammar and the results obtained are then addressed in section 5.

2 Multiword Expressions

The term Multiword Expressions (MWEs) has been used to describe expressions for which the syntactic or semantic properties of the whole expression cannot be derived from its parts ((Sag et al., 2002), (Villavicencio et al., 2005)), including a large number of related but distinct phenomena, such as phrasal verbs (e.g. *come along*), nominal compounds (e.g. *frying pan*), institutionalised phrases (e.g. *bread and butter*), and many others. They are used frequently in language, and in English, Jackendoff (1997) estimates the number of MWEs in a speaker's lexicon to be comparable to the number of single words. This is reflected in several existing grammars and lexical resources, where almost half of the entries are Multiword Expressions. However, due to their heterogeneous characteristics, MWEs present a tough challenge for both linguistic and computational work (Sag et al., 2002). Some MWEs are fixed, and do not present internal variation, such as *ad hoc*, while others allow different degrees of internal variability and modification, such as *touch a nerve* (*touch/find a nerve*) and *spill beans* (*spill several/musical/mountains of beans*). In terms of semantics, some MWEs are more opaque in their meaning (e.g. *to kick the bucket* as *to die*), while others have more transparent meanings that can be inferred from the words in the MWE (e.g. *eat up*, where the particle *up* adds a completive sense to *eat*). Therefore, to provide a unified account for the detection of these distinct but related phenomena is a real challenge for NLP systems.

3 Detection of Errors: Overview

van Noord (2004) reports on various errors that have been discovered for the Dutch Alpino Grammar (Bouma et al., 2001) semi-automatically, using the Twente Nieuws Corpus. The idea pursued by van Noord (2004) has been to locate those n-grams in the input that might be the cause of parsing failure. By processing a huge amount of data, the parsability metrics briefly presented in section 1 have been used to successfully locate various errors introduced by the tokenizer, erroneous/incomplete lexical descriptions, frozen expressions with idiosyncratic syntax, or incomplete grammatical descriptions. However, the recovery of these errors has been shown to still require significant efforts from the grammar developer. Moreover, there is no concrete data given about the distribution of the different types of errors discovered.

As also mentioned before, among the n-grams that usually cause parse failures, there is a large number of missing MWEs in the lexicon such as phrasal verbs, collocations, compound nouns, frozen expressions (e.g. *by and large*, *centre of attention*, *put forward by*, etc).

For the purpose of the detection of MWEs, we are interested in seeing what the major types of error for a typical large-scale deep grammar are. In this context, we have run the error mining experiment reported by van Noord with the English Resource Grammar (ERG; (Flickinger, 2000))[1] and the British National Corpus 2.0 (BNC; (Burnard, 2000)).

We have used a subset of the BNC written component. The sentences in this collection contain no more than 20 words and only ASCII characters. That is about 1.8M distinct sentences.

These sentences have then be fed into an efficient HPSG parser (PET; (Callmeier, 2000)) with ERG loaded. The parser has been configured with a maximum edge number limit of 100K and has run in the *best-only* mode so that it does not exhaustively find all the possible parses. The result of each sentence is marked as one of the following four cases:

- P means at least one parse is found for the sentence;
- L means the parser halted after the morphological analysis and has not been able to construct any lexical item for the input token;
- N means the search has finished normally and there is no parse found for the sentence;
- E means the search has finished abnormally by exceeding the edge number limit.

It is interesting to notice that when the ambiguity packing mechanism (Oepen and Carroll, 2000) is used and the unpacking is turned off [2], E does not occur at all for our test corpus. Running the parsability checking over the entire collection of sentences has taken the parser less than 2 days on a 64bit machine with 3GHz CPU. The results are shown in Table 1.

Result	# Sentences	Percentage
P	644,940	35.80%
L	969,452	53.82%
N	186,883	10.38%

Table 1: Distribution of Parsing Results

¿From the results shown in Table 1, one can see that ERG has full lexical span for less than half of the sentences. For these sentences, about 80% are successfully parsed. These numbers show that the grammar coverage has a significant improvement as compared to results reported by Baldwin et al. (2004) and Zhang and Kordoni (2006), mainly attributed to the increase in the size of the lexicon and the new rules to handle punctuations and fragments.

Obviously, L indicates the unknown words in the input sentence. But for N, it is not clear where

[1] ERG is a large-scale HPSG grammar for English. In this paper, we have used the January 2006 release of the grammar.

[2] For the experiment of error mining, only the parsability checking is necessary. There is no need to record the exact parses.

and what kind of error has occurred. In order to pinpoint the errors, we used the error mining techniques proposed by van Noord (2004) on the grammar and corpus. We have taken the sentences marked as N (because the errors in L sentences are already determined) and calculate the word sequence parsabilities against the sentences marked as P. The frequency cut is set to be 5. The whole process has taken no more than 20 minutes, resulting in total the parsability scores for 35K n-grams (word sequences). The distribution of n-grams in length with parsability below 0.1 is shown in Table 2.

	Number	Percentage
uni-gram	798	20.84%
bi-gram	2,011	52.52%
tri-gram	937	24.47%

Table 2: Distribution of N-gram in Length in Error Mining Results ($R(x) < 0.1$)

Although pinpointing the problematic n-grams still does not tell us what the exact errors are, it does shed some light on the cause. From Table 2 we see quite a lot of uni-grams with low parsabilities. Table 3 gives some examples of the word sequences. By intuition, we make the bold assumption that the low parsability of uni-grams is caused by the missing appropriate lexical entries for the corresponding word.[3]

For the bi-grams and tri-grams, we do see a lot of cases where the error can be repaired by just adding a multiword lexical entry into the grammar.

N-gram	Count
professionals	248
the flat	62
indication of	21
tone of voice	19
as always is	7

Table 3: Some Examples of the N-grams in Error Mining Results

In order to distinguish those n-grams that can be added into the grammar as MWE lexical entries from the other cases, we propose to validate them using evidence collected from the World Wide Web.

[3]It has later been confirmed with the grammar developer that almost all of the errors detected by these low parsability uni-grams can be fixed by adding correct lexical entries.

4 Detection of MWEs and related constructions

Recently, many researchers have started using the World Wide Web as an extremely large corpus, since, as pointed out by Grefenstette (1999), the Web is the largest data set available for NLP ((Grefenstette, 1999), (Keller et al., 2002), (Kilgarriff and Grefenstette, 2003) and (Villavicencio, 2005)). For instance, Grefenstette employs the Web to do example-based machine translation of compounds from French into English. The method he employs would suffer considerably from data sparseness, if it were to rely only on corpus data. So for compounds that are sparse in the BNC he also obtains frequencies from the Web. The scale of the Web can help to minimise the problem of data sparseness, that is especially acute for MWEs, and Villavicencio (2005) uses the Web to find evidence to verify automatically generated VPCs. This work is built on these, in that we propose to employ the Web as a corpus, using frequencies collected from the Web to detect MWEs among the n-grams that cause parse failure. We concentrate on the 482 most frequent candidates, to verify t he method.

The candidate list has been pre-processed to remove systematic unrelated entries, like those including acronyms, names, dates and numbers, following Bouma and Villada (2002). Using Google as a search engine, we have looked for evidence on the Web for each of the candidate MWEs, that have occurred as an exact match in a webpage. For each candidate searched, Google has provided us with a measure of frequency in the form of the number of pages in which it appears. Table 4 shows the 10 most frequent candidates, and among these there are parts of formulae, frozen expressions and collocations. Table 5 on the other hand, shows the 10 least frequent candidates. From the total of candidates, 311 have been kept while the other have been discarded as noise.

A manual inspection of the candidates has revealed that indeed the list contains a large amount of MWEs and frozen expressions like *taking into account the*, *good and evil*, *by and large*, *put forward by* and *breach of contract*. Some of these cases, like *come into effect in*, have very specific subcategorisation requirements, and this is reflected by the presence of the prepositions *into and in* in the ngram. Other cases seem to be part of formulae, like *but also in*, as part of *not only X but*

Table 4: Top 10 Candidate Multiword Expressions

MWE	Pages	Entropy	Prob(%)
the burden of	36600000	0.366	79.4
and cost effective	34400000	0.372	70.7
the likes of	34400000	0.163	93.1
but also in	27100000	0.038	98.9
to bring together	25700000	0.086	96.6
points of view	24500000	0.017	99.6
and the more	23700000	0.512	61.5
with and without	23100000	0.074	97.4
can do for	22300000	0.003	99.9
taking into account the	22100000	0.009	99.6
but what about	21000000	0.045	98.7
the ultimate in	17400000	0.199	90.0

Table 5: Bottom 10 Candidate Multiword Expressions

MWE	Pages	Entropy	Prob (%)
stand by and	1350000	0.399	65.5
discharged from hospital	553000	0.001	99.9
shock of it	92300	0.541	44.6
was woken by	91400	0.001	99.9
telephone rang and	43700	0.026	99.2
glanced across at	36900	0.003	99.9
the citizens charter	22900	0.070	97.9
input is complete	13900	0.086	97.2
from of government	706	0.345	0.1
the to infinitive	561	0.445	1.4

also Y, but what about, and *the more the* (part of *the more the Yer*).

However, among the candidates there still remain those that are not genuine MWEs, like *of alcohol and* and *than that in*, which contain very frequent words that enable them to obtain a very high frequency count without being an MWE. Therefore, to detect these cases, the remainder of the candidates could be further analysed using some statistical techniques to try to distinguish them from the more likely MWEs among the candidates. This is done by Bouma and Villada (2002) who investigated some measures that have been used to identify certain kinds of MWEs, focusing on collocational prepositional phrases, and on the tests of mutual information, log likelihood and χ^2. One significant difference here is that this work is not constrained to a particular type of MWEs, but has to deal with them in general. Moreover, the statistical measures used by Bouma and Villada demand the knowledge of single word frequencies which can be a problem when using Google especially for common words like *of* and *a*.

In Tables 4 and 5 we present two alternative measures that combined can help to detect false candidates. The rational is similar to the statistical tests, without the need of searching for the frequency of each of the words that make up the MWE. We assume that if a candidate is just a result of the random occurrence of very frequent words most probably the order of the words in the ngram is not important. Therefore, given a candidate, such as *the likes of*, we measure the frequency of occurrence of all its permutations (e.g. *the of likes, likes the of, etc*) and we calculate the candidate's entropy as

$$S = -\frac{1}{\log N} \sum_{k=1}^{N} P_i \log P_i \qquad (2)$$

where P_i is the probability of occurrence of a given permutation, and N the total number of permutations. The entropy above defined has its maximum at $S = 1$ when all permutations are equally probably, which indicates a clear signature of a random nature. On the other hand, when order is very important and only a single configuration is allowed the entropy has its minimum, $S = 0$. An ngram with low entropy has good chances of being an MWE. A close inspection on Table 4 shows that the top two candidate ngrams have relatively high entropies (here we consider high entropy when $S > 0.3$). In the first case this can be explained by the fact that the word *the* can appear after the word *of* without compromising the MWE meaning as in *the burden of the job*. In the second case it shows that the real MWE is *cost effective* and the word *and* can be either in the beginning or in the end of the trigram. In fact for a trigram with only two acceptable permutations the entropy is $S = \log 2/ \log 6 \simeq 0.39$, very close to what is obtained .

We also show the probability of occurrence of each candidate ngram among its permutations (P_1). Most of the candidates in the list are more frequent than their permutations. In Table 4 we find two exceptions which are clearly spelling errors in the last 2 ngrams. Therefore low P_1 can be a good indicative of a noisy candidate. Another good predictor is the relative frequency between the candidates. Given the occurrence values for the most frequent candidates, we consider that by using a threshold of 20,000 occurrences, it is possible to remove the more noisy cases.

We note that the grammar can also impose some restrictions in the order of the elements in the ngram, in the sense that some of the generated permutations are ungrammatical (e.g. *the of likes*) and will most probably have null or very low frequencies. Therefore, on top of the constraints on the lexical order there are also constraints on the constituent order of a candidate which will be reflected in these measures.[4]

The remainder candidates can be semi-automatically included in the grammar, by using a lexical type predictor, as described in the next section. With this information, each candidate is added as a lexical entry, with a possible manual check by a grammar writer prior to inclusion in the grammar.

[4]Google ignores punctuation between the elements of the ngram. This can lead to some hits being returned for some of the ungrammatical permuted ngrams, such as *one one by* in the sentence *We're going to catch people one by one. One day,...* from www.beertravelers.com/lists/drafttech.html. On the other hand, Google only returns the number of pages where a given ngram occurred, but not the number of times it occurred in that page. This can result in a huge underestimation especially for very frequent ngrams and words, which can be used mo re than once in a given page. Therefore, a conservative view of these frequencies must be adopted, given that for some ngrams they might be inflated and for others deflated.

5 Automated Deep Lexical Acquisition

In section (3), we have seen that more than 50% of the sentences contain one or more unknown words. And about half of the other parsing failures are also due to lexicon missing. In this section, we propose a statistical approach towards lexical type prediction for unknown words, including multiword expressions.

5.1 Atomic Lexical Types

Lexicalist grammars are normally composed of a limited number of rules and a lexicon with rich linguistic features attached to each entry. Some grammar formalisms have a type inheriting system to encode various constraints, and a flat structure of the lexicon with each entry mapped onto one type in the inheritance hierarchy. The following discussion is based on *Head-driven Phrase Structure Grammar (HPSG)* (Pollard and Sag, 1994), but should be easily adapted to other formalisms, as well.

The lexicon of HPSG consists of a list of well-formed *Typed Feature Structures (TFSs)* (Carpenter, 1992), which convey the constraints on specific words by two ways: the type compatibility, and the feature-value consistency. Although it is possible to use both features and types to convey the constraints on lexical entries, large grammars prefer the use of types in the lexicon because the inheritance system prevents the redundant definition of feature-values. And the feature-value constraints in the lexicon can be avoided by extending the types. Say we have n lexical entries $L_i : \left[\text{F} \;\; a_1\right]_t \dots L_n : \left[\text{F} \;\; a_n\right]_t$. They share the same lexical type t, but take different values for the feature F. If $a_1, \dots, a_n$ are the only possible values for F in the context of type t, we can extend the type t with subtypes $t_{a1} : \left[\text{F} \;\; a_1\right]_t \dots t_{an} : \left[\text{F} \;\; a_n\right]_t$ and modify the lexical entries to use these new types, respectively. Based on the fact that large grammars normally have a very restricted number of feature-values constraints for each lexical type, the increase of the types is acceptable. It is also typical that the types assigned to lexical entries are maximum on the type hierarchy, which means that they have no further subtypes. We will call the maximum lexical types after extension the *atomic lexical types*. Then the lexicon will be a multi-valued mapping from the word stems to the atomic lexical types.

Needless to underline here that all we have mentioned above is not applicable exclusively to HPSG, but to many other formalisms based on TFSs, which makes our assumptions about atomic lexical types all the more relevant for a wide range of systems and applications.

5.2 Statistical Lexical Type Predictor

Given that the lexicon of deep grammars can be modelled by a mapping from word stems to atomic lexical types, we now go on designing the statistical methods that can automatically "guess" such mappings for unknown words.

Similar to Baldwin (2005), we also treat the problem as a classification task. But there is an important difference. While Baldwin (2005) makes predictions for each unknown word, we create a new lexical entry for each occurrence of the unknown word. The assumption behind this is that there should be exactly one lexical entry that corresponds to the occurrence of the word in the given context[5].

We use a single classifier to predict the atomic lexical type. There are normally hundreds of atomic lexical types for a large grammar. So the classification model should be able to handle a large number of output classes. We choose the Maximum Entropy-based model because it can easily handle thousands of features and a large number of possible outputs. It also has the advantages of general feature representation and no independence assumption between features. With the efficient parameter estimation algorithms discussed by Malouf (2002), the training of the model is now very fast.

For our prediction model, the probability of a lexical type t given an unknown word and its context c is:

$$p(t|c) = \frac{exp(\sum_i \theta_i f_i(t,c))}{\sum_{t' \in T} exp(\sum_i \theta_i f_i(t',c))} \qquad (3)$$

where feature $f_i(t,c)$ may encode arbitrary characteristics of the context. The parameters $< \theta_1, \theta_2, \dots >$ can be evaluated by maximising the pseudo-likelihood on a training corpus (Malouf, 2002). The detailed design and feature selection for the lexical type predictor are described in Zhang and Kordoni (2006).

[5]Lexical ambiguity is not considered here for the unknowns. In principle, this constraint can be relaxed by allowing the classifier to return more than one results by, setting a confidence threshold, for example.

In the experiment described here, we have used the latest version of the Redwoods Treebank in order to train the lexical type predictor with morphological features and context words/POS tags features [6]. We have then extracted from the BNC 6248 sentences, which contain at least one of the 311 MWE candidates verified with World Wide Web in the way described in the previous section. For each occurrence of the MWE candidates in this set of sentences, our lexical type predictor has predicted a lexical entry candidate. This has resulted in 1936 distinct entries. Only those entries with at least 5 counts have been added into the grammar. This has resulted in an extra 373 MWE lexical entries for the grammar.

This addition to the grammar has resulted in a significant increase in coverage (table 6) of 14.4%. This result is very promising, as only a subset of the candidate MWEs has been analysed, and could result in an even greater increase in coverage, if these techniques were applied to the complete set of candidates.

However, we should also point out that the coverage numbers reported in Table 6 are for a set of "difficult" sentences which contains a lot of MWEs. When compared to the numbers reported in Table 1, the coverage of the parser on this data set after adding the MWE entries is still significantly lower. This indicates that not all the MWEs can be correctly handled by simply adding more lexical entries. Further investigation is still required.

6 Conclusions

One of the important challenges for robust natural language processing systems is to be able to deal with the systematic parse failures caused in great part by Multiword Expressions and related constructions. Therefore, in this paper we have proposed an approach for the semi-automatic extension of grammars by using an error mining technique for the detection of MWE candidates in texts and for predicting possible lexico-syntactic types for them. The approach presented is based on that of van Noord (2004) and proposes a set of MWE candidates. For this set of candidates, using the World Wide Web as a large corpus, frequencies are gathered for each candidate. These in conjunction with some statistical measures are employed for ruling out noisy cases like spelling mistakes (*from of government*) and frequent non-MWE sequences like *input is complete*.

With this information the remaining sequences are analysed by a statistical type predictor that assigns the most likely lexical type for each of the candidates in a given context. By adding these to the grammar as new lexical entries, a considerable increase in coverage of 14.4% was obtained.

The approach proposed employs simple and self-contained techniques that are language-independent and can help to semi-automatically extend the coverage of a grammar without relying on external resources, like electronic dictionaries and ontologies that are expensive to obtain and not available for all languages. Therefore, it provides an inexpensive and reusable manner of helping and speeding up the grammar engineering process, by relieving the grammar developer of some of the burden of extending the coverage of the grammar.

As future work we intend to investigate further statistical measures that can be applied robustly to different types of MWEs for refining even more the list of candidates and distinguishing false positives, like *of alcohol and* from MWEs, like *put forward by*. The high frequency with which the former occur in corpora and the more accute problem of data sparseness that affects the latter make this a difficult task.

[6] The POS tags are produced with the *TnT* tagger.

References

Timothy Baldwin, Emily M. Bender, Dan Flickinger, Ara Kim, and Stephan Oepen. 2004. Road-testing the English Resource Grammar over the British National Corpus. In *Proceedings of the Fourth International Conference on Language Resources and Evaluation (LREC 2004)*, Lisbon, Portugal.

Timothy Baldwin. 2005. Bootstrapping deep lexical resources: Resources for courses. In *Proceedings of the ACL-SIGLEX Workshop on Deep Lexical Acquisition*, pages 67–76, Ann Arbor, Michigan, June. Association for Computational Linguistics.

Gosse Bouma and Begoña Villada. 2002. Corpus-based acquisition of collocational prepositional phrases. In *Proceedings of the Computational Linguistics in the Netherlands (CLIN) 2001*, University of Twente.

Gosse Bouma, Gertjan van Noord, and Robert Malouf. 2001. Alpino: Wide-coverage computational analysis of dutch. In *Computational Linguistics in The Netherlands 2000.*

	Entries Added	Item #	Covered #	Coverage
ERG	0	6246	268	4.3%
ERG+MWE(Web)	373	6246	1168	18.7%

Table 6: Parser coverage on "difficult" sentences before/after adding MWE lexical entries

Lou Burnard. 2000. User Reference Guide for the British National Corpus. Technical report, Oxford University Computing Services.

M. Butt, S. Dipper, A. Frank, and T.H. King. 1999. Writing large-scale parallel grammars for english, french, and german. In *Proceedings of the LFG99 Conference*. CSLI Publications.

Ulrich Callmeier. 2000. PET – a platform for experimentation with efficient HPSG processing techniques. *Journal of Natural Language Engineering*, 6(1):99–108.

Bob Carpenter. 1992. *The Logic of Typed Feature Structures*. Cambridge University Press, Cambridge, England.

Dan Flickinger. 2000. On building a more efficient grammar by exploiting types. *Natural Language Engineering*, 6(1):15–28.

Gregory Grefenstette. 1999. The World Wide Web as a resource for example-based machine translation tasks. In *Proceedings of ASLIB, Conference on Translating and the Computer*, London.

Ray Jackendoff. 1997. Twistin' the night away. *Language*, 73:534–59.

Frank Keller, Maria Lapata, and Olga Ourioupina. 2002. Using the Web to overcome data sparseness. In Jan Hajič and Yuji Matsumoto, editors, *Proceedings of the Conference on Empirical Methods in Natural Language Processing*, pages 230–237, Philadelphia.

Adam Kilgarriff and Gregory Grefenstette. 2003. Introduction to the special issue on web as corpus. *Computational Linguistics*, 29.

Robert Malouf. 2002. A comparison of algorithms for maximum entropy parameter estimation. In *Proceedings of the Sixth Conferencde on Natural Language Learning (CoNLL-2002)*, pages 49–55.

Stephan Oepen and John Carroll. 2000. Ambiguity packing in constraint-based parsing — practical results. In *Proceedings of the 1st Conference of the North American Chapter of the ACL*, pages 162–169, Seattle, WA.

Carl J. Pollard and Ivan A. Sag. 1994. *Head-Driven Phrase Structure Grammar*. University of Chicago Press, Chicago, Illinois.

Ivan Sag, Timothy Baldwin, Francis Bond, Ann Copestake, and Dan Flickinger. 2002. Multiword expressions: A pain in the neck for NLP. In *Proceedings of the 3rd International Conference on Intelligent Text Processing and Computational Linguistics (CICLing-2002)*, pages 1–15, Mexico City, Mexico.

Gertjan van Noord. 2004. Error mining for wide-coverage grammar engineering. In *Proceedings of the 42nd Meeting of the Association for Computational Linguistics (ACL'04), Main Volume*, pages 446–453, Barcelona, Spain, July.

Aline Villavicencio, Francis Bond, Anna Korhonen, and Diana McCarthy. 2005. Introduction to the special issue on multiword expressions: having a crack at a hard nut. *Journal of Computer Speech and Language Processing*, 19.

Aline Villavicencio. 2005. The availability of verb-particle constructions in lexical resources: How much is enough? *Journal of Computer Speech and Language Processing*, 19.

Yi Zhang and Valia Kordoni. 2006. Automated deep lexical acquisition for robust open texts processing. In *Proceedings of the Fifth International Conference on Language Resources and Evaluation (LREC 2006)*, Genoa, Italy.

Classifying Particle Semantics in English Verb-Particle Constructions

Paul Cook
Department of Computer Science
University of Toronto
Toronto, ON M5S 3G4
Canada
pcook@cs.toronto.edu

Suzanne Stevenson
Department of Computer Science
University of Toronto
Toronto, ON M5S 3G4
Canada
suzanne@cs.toronto.edu

Abstract

Previous computational work on learning the semantic properties of verb-particle constructions (VPCs) has focused on their compositionality, and has left unaddressed the issue of *which* meaning of the component words is being used in a given VPC. We develop a feature space for use in classification of the sense contributed by the particle in a VPC, and test this on VPCs using the particle *up*. The features that capture linguistic properties of VPCs that are relevant to the semantics of the particle outperform linguistically uninformed word co-occurrence features in our experiments on unseen test VPCs.

1 Introduction

A challenge in learning the semantics of multiword expressions (MWEs) is their varying degrees of *compositionality*—the contribution of each component word to the overall semantics of the expression. MWEs fall on a range from fully compositional (i.e., each component contributes its meaning, as in *frying pan*) to non-compositional or idiomatic (as in *hit the roof*). Because of this variation, researchers have explored automatic methods for learning whether, or the degree to which, an MWE is compositional (e.g., Lin, 1999; Bannard et al., 2003; McCarthy et al., 2003; Fazly et al., 2005).

However, such work leaves unaddressed the basic issue of which of the possible meanings of a component word is contributed when the MWE is (at least partly) compositional. Words are notoriously ambiguous, so that even if it can be determined that an MWE is compositional, its meaning is still unknown, since the actual semantic contribution of the components is yet to be determined. We address this problem in the domain of verb-particle constructions (VPCs) in English, a rich source of MWEs.

VPCs combine a verb with any of a finite set of particles, as in *jump up*, *figure out*, or *give in*. Particles such as *up*, *out*, or *in*, with their literal meaning based in physical spatial relations, show a variety of metaphorical and aspectual meaning extensions, as exemplified here for the particle *up*:

(1a) The sun just <u>came up</u>. [vertical spatial movement]

(1b) She <u>walked up</u> to him. [movement toward a goal]

(1c) <u>Drink up</u> your juice! [completion]

(1d) He <u>curled up</u> into a ball. [reflexive movement]

Cognitive linguistic analysis, as in Lindner (1981), can provide the basis for elaborating this type of semantic variation.

Given such a sense inventory for a particle, our goal is to automatically determine its meaning when used with a given verb in a VPC. We classify VPCs according to their particle sense, using statistical features that capture the semantic and syntactic properties of verbs and particles. We contrast these with simple word co-occurrence features, which are often used to indicate the semantics of a target word. In our experiments, we focus on VPCs using the particle *up* because it is highly frequent and has a wide range of meanings. However, it is worth emphasizing that our feature space draws on general properties of VPCs, and is not specific to this particle.

A VPC may be ambiguous, with its particle occurring in more than one sense; in contrast to (1a), *come up* may use *up* in a goal-oriented sense as in

Proceedings of the Workshop on Multiword Expressions: Identifying and Exploiting Underlying Properties, pages 45–53, Sydney, July 2006.

The deadline is coming up. While our long-term goal is token classification (disambiguation) of a VPC in context, following other work on VPCs (e.g., Bannard et al., 2003; McCarthy et al., 2003), we begin here with the task of type classification. Given our use of features which capture the statistical behaviour relevant to a VPC across a corpus, we assume that the outcome of type classification yields the predominant sense of the particle in the VPC. Predominant sense identification is a useful component of sense disambiguation of word tokens (McCarthy et al., 2004), and we presume our VPC type classification work will form the basis for later token disambiguation.

Section 2 continues the paper with a discussion of the features we developed for particle sense classification. Section 3 first presents some brief cognitive linguistic background, followed by the sense classes of *up* used in our experiments. Sections 4 and 5 discuss our experimental set-up and results, Section 6 related work, and Section 7 our conclusions.

2 Features Used in Classification

The following subsections describe the two sets of features we investigated. The linguistic features are motivated by specific semantic and syntactic properties of verbs and VPCs, while the word co-occurrence features are more general.

2.1 Linguistically Motivated Features

2.1.1 Slot Features

We hypothesize that the semantic contribution of a particle when combined with a given verb is related to the semantics of that verb. That is, the particle contributes the same meaning when combining with any of a semantic class of verbs.[1] For example, the VPCs *drink up*, *eat up* and *gobble up* all draw on the completion sense of *up*; the VPCs *puff out*, *spread out* and *stretch out* all draw on the extension sense of *out*. The prevalence of these patterns suggests that features which have been shown to be effective for the semantic classification of verbs may be useful for our task.

We adopt simple syntactic "slot" features which have been successfully used in automatic semantic classification of verbs (Joanis and Stevenson, 2003). The features are motivated by the fact that semantic properties of a verb are reflected in the syntactic expression of the participants in the event the verb describes. The slot features encode the relative frequencies of the syntactic slots—subject, direct and indirect object, object of a preposition—that the arguments and adjuncts of a verb appear in. We calculate the slot features over three contexts: all uses of a verb; all uses of the verb in a VPC with the target particle (*up* in our experiments); all uses of the verb in a VPC with any of a set of high frequency particles (to capture its semantics when used in VPCs in general).

2.1.2 Particle Features

Two types of features are motivated by properties specific to the semantics and syntax of particles and VPCs. First, Wurmbrand (2000) notes that compositional particle verbs in German (a somewhat related phenomenon to English VPCs) allow the replacement of their particle with semantically similar particles. We extend this idea, hypothesizing that when a verb combines with a particle such as *up* in a particular sense, the pattern of usage of that verb in VPCs using all other particles may be indicative of the sense of the target particle (in this case *up*) when combined with that verb. To reflect this observation, we count the relative frequency of any occurrence of the verb used in a VPC with each of a set of high frequency particles.

Second, one of the striking syntactic properties of VPCs is that they can often occur in either the joined configuration (2a) or the split configuration (2b):

(2a) Drink up your milk! He walked out quickly.

(2b) Drink your milk up! He walked quickly out.

Bolinger (1971) notes that the joined construction may be more favoured when the sense of the particle is not literal. To encode this, we calculate the relative frequency of the verb co-occurring with the particle *up* with each of 0–5 words between the verb and *up*, reflecting varying degrees of verb-particle separation.

2.2 Word Co-occurrence Features

We also explore the use of general context features, in the form of word co-occurrence frequency vectors, which have been used in numerous approaches to determining the semantics of a target

[1] Villavicencio (2005) observes that verbs from a semantic class will form VPCs with similar sets of particles. Here we are hypothesizing further that VPCs formed from verbs of a semantic class draw on the same meaning of the given particle.

word. Note, however, that unlike the task of word sense disambiguation, which examines the context of a target word token to be disambiguated, here we are looking at aggregate contexts across all instances of a target VPC, in order to perform type classification.

We adopt very simple word co-occurrence features (WCFs), calculated as the frequency of any (non-stoplist) word within a certain window left and right of the target. We noted above that the target particle semantics is related both to the semantics of the verb it co-occurs with, and to the occurrence of the verb across VPCs with different particles. Thus we not only calculate the WCFs of the target VPC (a given verb used with the particle *up*), but also the WCFs of the verb itself, and the verb used in a VPC with any of the high frequency particles. These WCFs give us a very general means for determining semantics, whose performance we can contrast with our linguistic features.

3 Particle Semantics and Sense Classes

We give some brief background on cognitive grammar and its relation to particle semantics, and then turn to the semantic analysis of *up* that we draw on as the basis for the sense classes in our experiments.

3.1 Cognitive Grammar and Schemas

Some linguistic studies consider many VPCs to be idiomatic, but do not give a detailed account of the semantic similarities between them (Bolinger, 1971; Fraser, 1976; Jackendoff, 2002). In contrast, work in cognitive linguistics has claimed that many so-called idiomatic expressions draw on the compositional contribution of (at least some of) their components (Lindner, 1981; Morgan, 1997; Hampe, 2000). In cognitive grammar (Langacker, 1987), non-spatial concepts are represented as spatial relations. Key terms from this framework are:

Trajector (TR) The object which is conceptually foregrounded.

Landmark (LM) The object against which the TR is foregrounded.

Schema An abstract conceptualization of an experience. Here we focus on schemas depicting a TR, LM and their relationship in both the initial configuration and the final configuration communicated by some expression.

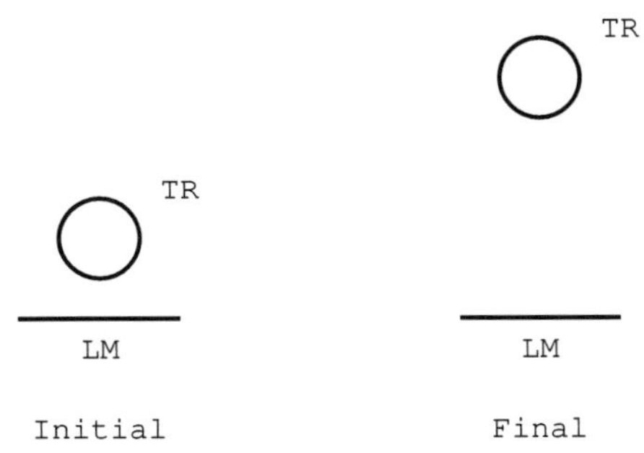

Figure 1: Schema for Vertical *up*.

The semantic contribution of a particle in a VPC corresponds to a schema. For example, in sentence (3), the TR is the balloon and the LM is the ground the balloon is moving away from.

(3) The balloon floated up.

The schema describing the semantic contribution of the particle in the above sentence is shown in Figure 1, which illustrates the relationship between the TR and LM in the initial and final configurations.

3.2 The Senses of *up*

Lindner (1981) identifies a set of schemas for each of the particles *up* and *out*, and groups VPCs according to which schema is contributed by their particle. Here we describe the four senses of *up* identified by Lindner.

3.2.1 Vertical *up* (Vert-*up*)

In this schema (shown above in Figure 1), the TR moves away from the LM in the direction of increase along a vertically oriented axis. This includes prototypical spatial upward movement such as that in sentence (3), as well as upward movement along an abstract vertical axis as in sentence (4).

(4) The price of gas jumped up.

In Lindner's analysis, this sense also includes extensions of upward movement where a vertical path or posture is still salient. Note that in some of these senses, the notion of verticality is metaphorical; the contribution of such senses to a VPC may not be considered compositional in a traditional analysis. Some of the most common sense extensions are given below, with a brief justification as to why verticality is still salient.

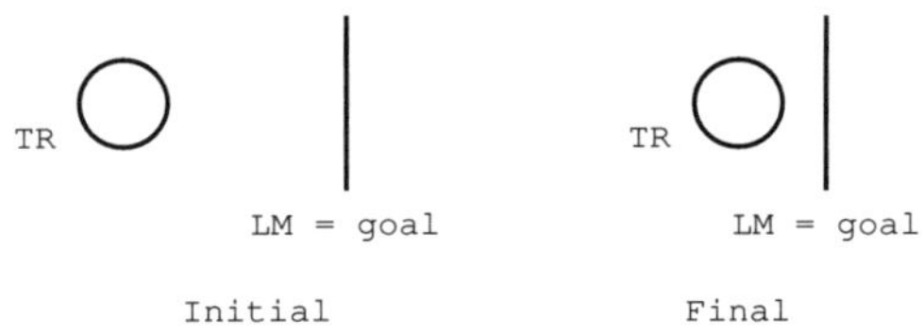

Figure 2: Schema for Goal-Oriented *up*.

Up as a path into perceptual field. Spatially high objects are generally easier to perceive. Examples: *show up*, *spring up*, *whip up*.

Up as a path into mental field. Here *up* encodes a path for mental as opposed to physical objects. Examples: *dream up*, *dredge up*, *think up*.

Up as a path into a state of activity. Activity is prototypically associated with an erect posture. Examples: *get up*, *set up*, *start up*.

3.2.2 Goal-Oriented *up* (Goal-*up*)

Here the TR approaches a goal LM; movement is not necessarily vertical (see Figure 2). Prototypical examples are *walk up* and *march up*. This category also includes extensions into the social domain (*kiss up* and *suck up*), as well as extensions into the domain of time (*come up* and *move up*), as in:

(5a) The intern kissed up to his boss.

(5b) The deadline is coming up quickly.

3.2.3 Completive *up* (Cmpl-*up*)

Cmpl-*up* is a sub-sense of Goal-*up* in which the goal represents an action being done to completion. This sense shares its schema with Goal-*up* (Figure 2), but it is considered as a separate sense since it corresponds to uses of *up* as an aspectual marker. Examples of Cmpl-*up* are: *clean up*, *drink up*, *eat up*, *finish up* and *study up*.

3.2.4 Reflexive *up* (Refl-*up*)

Reflexive *up* is a sub-sense of Goal-*up* in which the sub-parts of the TR are approaching each other. The schema for Refl-*up* is shown in Figure 3; it is unique in that the TR and LM are the same object. Examples of Refl-*up* are: *bottle up*, *connect up*, *couple up*, *curl up* and *roll up*.

Figure 3: Schema for Reflexive *up*.

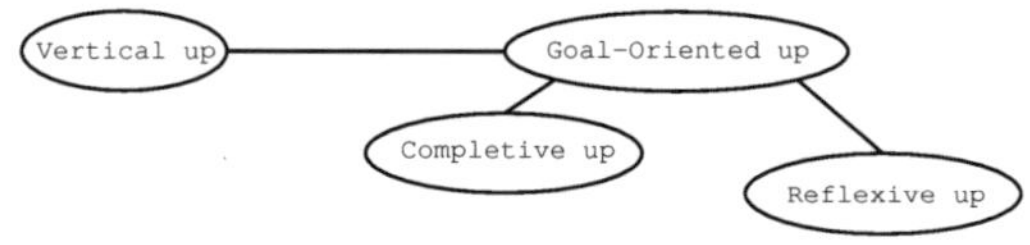

Figure 4: Simplified schematic network for *up*.

3.3 The Sense Classes for Our Study

Adopting a cognitive linguistic perspective, we assume that all uses of a particle make some compositional contribution of meaning to a VPC. In this work, we classify target VPCs according to which of the above senses of *up* is contributed to the expression. For example, the expressions *jump up* and *pick up* are designated as being in the class Vert-*up* since *up* in these VPCs has the vertical sense, while *clean up* and *drink up* are designated as being in the class Cmpl-*up* since *up* here has the completive sense. The relations among the senses of *up* can be shown in a "schematic network" (Langacker, 1987). Figure 4 shows a simplification of such a network in which we connect more similar senses with shorter edges. This type of analysis allows us to alter the granularity of our classification in a linguistically motivated fashion by combining closely related senses. Thus we can explore the effect of different sense granularities on classification.

4 Materials and Methods

4.1 Experimental Expressions

We created a list of English VPCs using *up*, based on a list of VPCs made available by McIntyre (2001) and a list of VPCs compiled by two human judges. The judges then filtered this list to include only VPCs which they both agreed were valid, resulting in a final list of 389 VPCs. From this list, training, verification and test sets of sixty VPCs each are randomly selected. Note that the expense of manually annotating the data (as described below) prevents us from using larger datasets in this initial investigation. The experimental sets are chosen such that each includes the same proportion of verbs across three frequency bands, so that the sets do not differ in frequency distribution of the verbs. (We use frequency of the verbs, rather than the VPCs, since many of our features are based on the verb of the expression, and moreover, VPC frequency is approximate.) The verification data is used in exploration of the feature space and selection of final features to use in testing; the test set is held out for final testing of the classifiers.

Each VPC in each dataset is annotated by the two human judges according to which of the four senses of *up* identified in Section 3.2 is contributed to the VPC. As noted in Section 1, VPCs may be ambiguous with respect to their particle sense. Since our task here is type classification, the judges identify the particle sense of a VPC in its predominant usage, in their assessment. The observed inter-annotator agreement is 0.80 for each dataset. The unweighted observed kappa scores are 0.73, 0.64 and 0.55, for the training, verification and test sets respectively.

4.2 Calculation of the Features

We extract our features from the 100M word British National Corpus (BNC, Burnard, 2000). VPCs are identified using a simple heuristic based on part-of-speech tags, similar to one technique used by Baldwin (2005). A use of a verb is considered a VPC if it occurs with a particle (tagged AVP) within a six word window to the right. Over a random sample of 113 VPCs thus extracted, we found 88% to be true VPCs, somewhat below the performance of Baldwin's (2005) best extraction method, indicating potential room for improvement.

The slot and particle features are calculated using a modified version of the ExtractVerb software provided by Joanis and Stevenson (2003), which runs over the BNC pre-processed using Abney's (1991) Cass chunker.

To compute the word co-occurrence features (WCFs), we first determine the relative frequency of all words which occur within a five word window left and right of any of the target expressions in the training data. From this list we eliminate the most frequent 1% of words as a stoplist and then use the next n most frequent words as "feature words". For each "feature word", we then calculate its relative frequency of occurrence within the same five word window of the target expressions in all datasets. We use $n = 200$ and $n = 500$ to create feature sets WCF_{200} and WCF_{500} respectively.

	#VPCs in Sense Class		
Sense Class	Train	Verification	Test
Vert-*up*	24	33	27
Goal-*up*	1	1	3
Cmpl-*up*	20	23	22
Refl-*up*	15	3	8

Table 1: Frequency of items in each sense class.

	#VPCs in Sense Class		
Sense Class	Train	Verification	Test
Vert-*up*	24	33	27
Goal-*up* + Cmpl-*up*	21	24	25
Refl-*up*	15	3	8

Table 2: Frequency of items in each class for the 3-way task.

4.3 Experimental Classes

Table 1 shows the distribution of senses in each dataset. Each of the training and verification sets has only one VPC corresponding to Goal-*up*. Recall that Goal-*up* shares a schema with Cmpl-*up*, and is therefore very close to it in meaning, as indicated spatially in Figure 4. We therefore merge Goal-*up* and Cmpl-*up* into a single sense, to provide more balanced classes.

Since we want to see how our features perform on differing granularities of sense classes, we run each experiment as both a 3-way and 2-way classification task. In the 3-way task, the sense classes correspond to the meanings Vert-*up*, Goal-*up* merged with Cmpl-*up* (as noted above), and Refl-*up*, as shown in Table 2. In the 2-way task, we further merge the classes corresponding to Goal-

	#VPCs in Sense Class		
Sense Class	Train	Verification	Test
Vert-*up*	24	33	27
Goal-*up* + Cmpl-*up* + Refl-*up*	36	27	33

Table 3: Frequency of items in each class for the 2-way task.

up/Cmpl-*up* with that of Refl-*up*, as shown in Table 3. We choose to merge these classes because (as illustrated in Figure 4) Refl-*up* is a sub-sense of Goal-*up*, and moreover, all three of these senses contrast with Vert-*up*, in which increase along a vertical axis is the salient property. It is worth emphasizing that the 2-way task is not simply a classification between literal and non-literal *up*—Vert-*up* includes extensions of *up* in which the increase along a vertical axis is metaphorical.

4.4 Evaluation Metrics and Classifier Software

The variation in the frequency of the sense classes of *up* across the datasets makes the true distribution of the classes difficult to estimate. Furthermore, there is no obvious informed baseline for this task. Therefore, we make the assumption that the true distribution of the classes is uniform, and use the chance accuracy $1/C$ as the baseline (where C is the number of classes—in our experiments, either 2 or 3). Accordingly, our measure of classification accuracy should weight each class evenly. Therefore, we report the average per class accuracy, which gives equal weight to each class.

For classification we use LIBSVM (Chang and Lin, 2001), an implementation of a support-vector machine. We set the input parameters, cost and gamma, using 10-fold cross-validation on the training data. In addition, we assign a weight of $\frac{|Largest\ Class|}{|Class\ c|}$ to each class c to eliminate the effects of the variation in class size on the classifier.

Note that our choice of accuracy measure and weighting of classes in the classifier is necessary given our assumption of a uniform random baseline. Since the accuracy values we report incorporate this weighting, these results cannot be compared to a baseline of always choosing the most frequent class.

5 Experimental Results

We present experimental results for both Ver(ification) and unseen Test data, on each set of features, individually and in combination. All experiments are run on both the 2-way and 3-way sense classification, which have a chance baseline of 50% and 33%, respectively.

	3-way Task		2-way Task	
Features	Ver	Test	Ver	Test
Slots	41	51	53	67
Particles	37	33	65	47
Slots + Particles	54	54	59	63

Table 4: Accuracy (%) using linguistic features.

5.1 Experiments Using the Linguistic Features

The results for experiments using the features that capture semantic and syntactic properties of verbs and VPCs are summarized in Table 4, and discussed in turn below.

5.1.1 Slot Features

Experiments using the slot features alone test whether features that tap into semantic information about a verb are sufficient to determine the appropriate sense class of a particle when that verb combines with it in a VPC. Although accuracy on the test data is well above the baseline in both the 2-way and 3-way tasks, for verification data the increase over the baseline is minimal. The class corresponding to sense Refl-*up* in the 3-way task is relatively small, which means that a small variation in classification on these verbs may lead to a large variation in accuracy. However, we find that the difference in accuracy across the datasets is not due to performance on VPCs in this sense class. Although these features show promise for our task, the variation across the datasets indicates the limitations of our small sample sizes.

5.1.2 Particle Features

We also examine the performance of the particle features on their own, since to the best of our knowledge, no such features have been used before in investigating VPCs. The results are disappointing, with only the verification data on the 2-way task showing substantially higher accuracy than the baseline. An analysis of errors reveals no consistent explanation, suggesting again that the variation may be due to small sample sizes.

5.1.3 Slot + Particle Features

We hypothesize that the combination of the slot features with the particle features will give an increase in performance over either set of linguistic features used individually, given that they tap into differing properties of verbs and VPCs. We find that the combination does indeed give more

Features	3-way Task Ver	3-way Task Test	2-way Task Ver	2-way Task Test
WCF_{200}	45	42	59	51
WCF_{500}	38	34	55	48

Table 5: Accuracy (%) using WCFs.

Features	3-way Task Ver	3-way Task Test	2-way Task Ver	2-way Task Test
$Combined_{200}$	53	45	63	53
$Combined_{500}$	54	46	65	49

Table 6: Accuracy (%) combining linguistic features with WCFs.

consistent performance across verification and test data than either feature set used individually. We analyze the errors made using slot and particle features separately, and find that they tend to classify different sets of verbs incorrectly. Therefore, we conclude that these feature sets are at least somewhat complementary. By combining these complementary feature sets, the classifier is better able to generalise across different datasets.

5.2 Experiments Using WCFs

Our goal was to compare the more knowledge-rich slot and particle features to an alternative feature set, the WCFs, which does not rely on linguistic analysis of the semantics and syntax of verbs and VPCs. Recall that we experiment with both 200 feature words, WCF_{200}, and 500 feature words, WCF_{500}, as shown in Table 5. Most of the experiments using WCFs perform worse than the corresponding experiment using all the linguistic features. It appears that the linguistically motivated features are better suited to our task than simple word context features.

5.3 Linguistic Features and WCFs Combined

Although the WCFs on their own perform worse than the linguistic features, we find that the linguistic features and WCFs are at least somewhat complementary since they tend to classify different verbs incorrectly. We hypothesize that, as with the slot and particle features, the different types of information provided by the linguistic features and WCFs may improve performance in combination. We therefore combine the linguistic features with each of the WCF_{200} and WCF_{500} features; see Table 6. However, contrary to our hypothesis, for the most part, the experiments using the full combination of features give accuracies the same or below that of the corresponding experiment using just the linguistic features. We surmise that these very different types of features—the linguistic features and WCFs—must be providing conflicting rather than complementary information to the classifier, so that no improvement is attained.

5.4 Discussion of Results

The best performance across the datasets is attained using all the linguistic features. The linguistically uninformed WCFs perform worse on their own, and do not consistently help (and in some cases hurt) the performance of the linguistic features when combined with them. We conclude then that linguistically based features are motivated for this task. Note that the features are still quite simple, and straightforward to extract from a corpus—i.e., linguistically informed does not mean expensive (although the slot features do require access to chunked text).

Interestingly, in determining the semantic nearest neighbor of German particle verbs, Schulte im Walde (2005) found that WCFs that are *restricted* to the arguments of the verb outperform simple window-based co-occurrence features. Although her task is quite different from ours, similarly restricting our WCFs may enable them to encode more linguistically-relevant information.

The accuracies we achieve with the linguistic features correspond to a 30–31% reduction in error rate over the chance baseline for the 3-way task, and an 18–26% reduction in error rate for the 2-way task. Although we expected that the 2-way task may be easier, since it requires less fine-grained distinctions, it is clear that combining senses that have some motivation for being treated separately comes at a price.

The reductions in error rate that we achieve with our best features are quite respectable for a first attempt at addressing this problem, but more work clearly remains. There is a relatively high variability in performance across the verification and test sets, indicating that we need a larger number of experimental expressions to be able to draw firmer conclusions. Even if our current results extend to larger datasets, we intend to explore other feature approaches, such as word co-occurrence features for specific syntactic slots as suggested above, in order to improve the performance.

6 Related Work

The semantic compositionality of VPC types has recently received increasing attention. McCarthy et al. (2003) use several measures to automatically rate the overall compositionality of a VPC. Bannard (2005), extending work by Bannard et al. (2003), instead considers the extent to which the verb and particle each contribute semantically to the VPC. In contrast, our work assumes that the particle of every VPC contributes compositionally to its meaning. We draw on cognitive linguistic analysis that posits a rich set of literal and metaphorical meaning possibilities of a particle, which has been previously overlooked in computational work on VPCs.

In this first investigation of particle meaning in VPCs, we choose to focus on type-based classification, partly due to the significant extra expense of manually annotating sufficient numbers of tokens in text. As noted earlier, though, VPCs can take on different meanings, indicating a shortcoming of type-based work. Patrick and Fletcher (2005) classify VPC tokens, considering each as compositional, non-compositional or not a VPC. Again, however, it is important to recognize *which* of the possible meaning components is being contributed. In this vein, Uchiyama et al. (2005) tackle token classification of Japanese compound verbs (similar to VPCs) as aspectual, spatial, or adverbial. In the future, we aim to extend the scope of our work, to determine the meaning of a particle in a VPC token, along the lines of our sense classes here. This will almost certainly require semantic classification of the verb token (Lapata and Brew, 2004), similar to our approach here of using the semantic class of a verb type as indicative of the meaning of a particle type.

Particle semantics has clear relations to preposition semantics. Some research has focused on the sense disambiguation of specific prepositions (e.g., Alam, 2004), while other work has classified preposition tokens according to their semantic role (O'Hara and Wiebe, 2003). Moreover, two large lexical resources of preposition senses are currently under construction, The Preposition Project (Litkowski, 2005) and PrepNet (Saint-Dizier, 2005). These resources were not suitable as the basis for our sense classes because they do not address the range of metaphorical extensions that a preposition/particle can take on, but future work may enable larger scale studies of the type needed to adequately address VPC semantics.

7 Conclusions

While progress has recently been made in techniques for assessing the compositionality of VPCs, work thus far has left unaddressed the problem of determining the particular meaning of the components. We focus here on the semantic contribution of the particle—a part-of-speech whose semantic complexity and range of metaphorical meaning extensions has been largely overlooked in prior computational work. Drawing on work within cognitive linguistics, we annotate a set of 180 VPCs according to the sense class of the particle *up*, our experimental focus in this initial investigation. We develop features that capture linguistic properties of VPCs that are relevant to the semantics of particles, and show that they outperform linguistically uninformed word co-occurrence features, achieving around 20–30% reduction in error rate over a chance baseline. Areas of on-going work include development of a broader range of features, consideration of methods for token-based semantic determination, and creation of larger experimental datasets.

References

S. Abney. 1991. Parsing by chunks. In R. Berwick, S. Abney, and C. Tenny, editors, *Principle-Based Parsing: Computation and Psycholinguistics*, p. 257–278. Kluwer Academic Publishers.

Y. S. Alam. 2004. Decision trees for sense disambiguation of prepositions: Case of over. In *HLT-NAACL 2004: Workshop on Computational Lexical Semantics*, p. 52–59.

T. Baldwin. 2005. The deep lexical acquisition of English verb-particle constructions. *Computer Speech and Language, Special Issue on Multiword Expressions*, 19(4):398–414.

C. Bannard. 2005. Learning about the meaning of verb-particle constructions from corpora. *Computer Speech and Language, Special Issue on Multiword Expressions*, 19(4):467–478.

C. Bannard, T. Baldwin, and A. Lascarides. 2003. A statistical approach to the semantics of verb-particles. In *Proceedings of the ACL-2003 Workshop on Multiword Expressions: Analysis, Acquisition and Treatment*, p. 65–72.

D. Bolinger. 1971. *The Phrasal Verb in English*. Harvard University Press.

L. Burnard. 2000. *The British National Corpus Users Reference Guide*. Oxford University Computing Services.

C.-C. Chang and C.-J. Lin. 2001. *LIBSVM: a library for support vector machines*. Software available at `http://www.csie.ntu.edu.tw/~cjlin/libsvm`.

A. Fazly, R. North, and S. Stevenson. 2005. Automatically distinguishing literal and figurative usages of highly polysemous verbs. In *Proceedings of the ACL-2005 Workshop on Deep Lexical Acquisition*.

B. Fraser. 1976. *The Verb-Particle Combination in English*. Academic Press.

B. Hampe. 2000. Facing up to the meaning of 'face up to': A cognitive semantico-pragmatic analysis of an English verb-particle construction. In A. Foolen and F. van der Leek, editors, *Constructions in Cognitive Linguistics. Selected Papers from the fifth International Cognitive Linguistics Conference*, p. 81–101. John Benjamins Publishing Company.

R. Jackendoff. 2002. English particle constructions, the lexicon, and the autonomy of syntax. In N. Dehe, R. Jackendoff, A. McIntyre, and S. Urban, editors, *Verb-Particle Explorations*. Mouton de Gruyter.

E. Joanis and S. Stevenson. 2003. A general feature space for automatic verb classification. In *Proceedings of the Conference of the European Chapter of the Association for Computational Linguistics (EACL-2003)*, p. 163–170.

R. W. Langacker. 1987. *Foundations of Cognitive Grammar: Theoretical Prerequisites*, volume 1. Stanford University Press, Stanford.

M. Lapata and C. Brew. 2004. Verb class disambiguation using informative priors. *Computational Linguistics*, 30(1):45–73.

D. Lin. 1999. Automatic identification of non-compositional phrases. In *Proceedings of the 37th Annual Meeting of the Association for Computational Linguistics*, p. 317–324.

S. Lindner. 1981. *A lexico-semantic analysis of English verb particle constructions with out and up*. Ph.D. thesis, University of California, San Diego.

K. C. Litkowski. 2005. The Preposition Project. In *Proceedings of the Second ACL-SIGSEM Workshop on the Linguistic Dimensions of Prepositions and their Use in Computational Linguistics Formalisms and Applications*.

D. McCarthy, B. Keller, and J. Carroll. 2003. Detecting a continuum of compositionality in phrasal verbs. In *Proceedings of the ACL-SIGLEX Workshop on Multiword Expressions: Analysis, Acquisition and Treatment*.

D. McCarthy, R. Koeling, J. Weeds, and J. Carroll. 2004. Finding predominant word senses in untagged text. In *Proceedings of the 42nd Annual Meeting of the Association for Computational Linguistics*, p. 280–287.

A. McIntyre. 2001. *The particle verb list*. `http://www.uni-leipzig.de/~angling/mcintyre/pv.list.pdf`.

P. S. Morgan. 1997. Figuring out *figure out*: Metaphor and the semantics of the English verb-particle construction. *Cognitive Linguistics*, 8(4):327–357.

T. O'Hara and J. Wiebe. 2003. Preposition semantic classification via Penn Treebank and FrameNet. In *Proceedings of CoNLL-2003*, p. 79–86.

J. Patrick and J. Fletcher. 2005. Classifying verb-particle constructions by verb arguments. In *Proceedings of the Second ACL-SIGSEM Workshop on the Linguistic Dimensions of Prepositions and their use in Computational Linguistics Formalisms and Applications*, p. 200–209.

P. Saint-Dizier. 2005. PrepNet: a framework for describing prepositions: Preliminary investigation results. In *Proceedings of the Sixth International Workshop on Computational Semantics (IWCS'05)*, p. 145–157.

S. Schulte im Walde. 2005. Exploring features to identify semantic nearest neighbours: A case study on German particle verbs. In *Proceedings of the International Conference on Recent Advances in Natural Language Processing*.

K. Uchiyama, T. Baldwin, and S. Ishizaki. 2005. Disambiguating Japanese compound verbs. *Computer Speech and Language, Special Issue on Multiword Expressions*, 19(4):497–512.

A. Villavicencio. 2005. The availability of verb-particle constructions in lexical resources: How much is enough? *Computer Speech and Language, Special Issue on Multiword Expressions*, 19(4):415–432.

S. Wurmbrand. 2000. The structure(s) of particle verbs. Master's thesis, McGill University.

Interpretation of Compound Nominalisations using Corpus and Web Statistics

Jeremy Nicholson and Timothy Baldwin
Department of Computer Science and Software Engineering
University of Melbourne, VIC 3010, Australia
and
NICTA Victoria Research Laboratories
University of Melbourne, VIC 3010, Australia
{jeremymn,tim}@csse.unimelb.edu.au

Abstract

We present two novel paraphrase tests for automatically predicting the inherent semantic relation of a given compound nominalisation as one of subject, direct object, or prepositional object. We compare these to the usual verb–argument paraphrase test using corpus statistics, and frequencies obtained by scraping the Google search engine interface. We also implemented a more robust statistical measure than maximum likelihood estimation — the confidence interval. A significant reduction in data sparseness was achieved, but this alone is insufficient to provide a substantial performance improvement.

1 Introduction

Compound nouns are a class of multiword expression (MWE) that have been of interest in recent computational linguistic work, as any task with a lexical semantic dimension (like machine translation or information extraction) must take into account their semantic markedness. A compound noun is a sequence of two or more nouns comprising an $\bar{N}$, for example, *polystyrene garden-gnome*. The productivity of compound nouns makes their treatment equally desirable and difficult. They appear frequently: more than 1% of the words in the British National Corpus (BNC: Burnard (2000)) participate in noun compounds (Tanaka and Baldwin, 2003). However, unestablished compounds are common: almost 70% of compounds identified in the BNC co-occur with a frequency of only one (Lapata and Lascarides, 2003).

Analysis of the entire space of compound nouns has been hampered to some degree as the space defies some regular set of predicates to define the implicit semantics between a modifier and its head. This semantic underspecification led early analysis to be primarily of a semantic nature, but more recent work has advanced into using syntax to predict the semantics, in the spirit of the study by Levin (1993) on diathesis alternations.

In this work, we examine compound nominalisations, a subset of compound nouns where the head has a morphologically–related verb. For example, *product replacement* has an underlying verbal head *replace*, whereas *garden-gnome* has no such form. While compound nouns in general have a set of semantic relationships between the head and modifier that is potentially non-finite, compound nominalisations are better defined, in that the modifier fills a syntactic argument relation with respect to the head. For example, *product* might fill the direct object slot of the verb *to replace* for the compound above. Compound nominalisations comprise a substantial minority of compound nouns, with figures of about 35% being observed (Grover et al., 2005; Nicholson, 2005).

We propose two novel paraphrases for a corpus statistical approach to predicting the relationship for a set of compound nominalisations, and investigate how using the World Wide Web as a corpus alleviates the common phenomenon of data sparseness, and how the volume of data impacts on the classification results. We also examine a more robust statistical approach to interpretation of the statistics than maximum likelihood estimates, called the confidence interval.

The rest of the paper is structured as follows: in Section 2, we present a brief background for our work, with a listing of our resources in Section 3. We detail our proposed method in Section 4, the corresponding results in Section 5, with a discus-

Proceedings of the Workshop on Multiword Expressions: Identifying and Exploiting Underlying Properties, pages 54–61,
Sydney, July 2006.

sion in Section 6 and a brief conclusion in Section 7.

2 Background

2.1 Compound Noun Interpretation

Compound nouns were seminally and thoroughly analysed by Levi (1978), who hand–constructs a nine–way set of semantic relations that she identifies as broadly defining the observed relationships between the compound head and modifier. Warren (1978) also inspects the syntax of compound nouns, to create a somewhat different set of twelve conceptual categories.

Early attempts to automatically classify compound nouns have taken a semantic approach: Finin (1980) and Isabelle (1984) use "role nominals" derived from the head of the compound to fill a slot with the modifier. Vanderwende (1994) uses a rule–based technique that scores a compound on possible semantic interpretations, while Jones (1995) implements a graph–based unification procedure over semantic feature structures for the head. Finally, Rosario and Hearst (2001) make use of a domain–specific lexical resource to classify according to neural networks and decision trees.

Syntactic classification, using paraphrasing, was first used by Leonard (1984), who uses a prioritised rule–based approach across a number of possible readings. Lauer (1995) employs a corpus statistical model over a similar paraphrase set based on prepositions. Lapata (2002) and Grover et al. (2005) again use a corpus statistical paraphrase–based approach, but with verb–argument relations for compound nominalisations — attempting to define the relation as one of subject, direct object, or a number of prepositional objects in the latter.

2.2 Web–as–Corpus Approaches

Using the World Wide Web for corpus statistics is a relatively recent phenomenon, we present a few notable examples. Grefenstette (1998) analyses the plausibility of candidate translations in a machine translation task through Web statistics, and avoids some data sparseness within that context. Zhu and Rosenfeld (2001) train a language model from a large corpus, and use the Web to estimate low–density trigram frequencies. Keller and Lapata (2003) show that Web counts can obviate data sparseness for syntactic predicate–argument bigrams. They also observe that the noisiness of the Web, while unexplored in detail, does not greatly reduce the reliability of their results. Nakov and Hearst (2005) demonstrate that Web counts can aid in identifying the bracketing in higher–arity noun compounds. Finally, Lapata and Keller (2005) evaluate the performance of Web counts on a wide range of natural language processing tasks, including compound noun bracketing and compound noun interpretation.

2.3 Confidence Intervals

Maximum likelihood statistics are not robust when many sparse vectors are under consideration, i.e. naively "choosing the largest number" may not be accurate in contexts when the relative value across samplings may be relevant, for example, in machine learning. As such, we apply a statistical test with confidence intervals (Kenney and Keeping, 1962), where we compare sample z-scores in a pairwise manner, instead of frequencies globally.

The confidence interval P, for z-score n, is:

$$P = \frac{2}{\sqrt{\pi}} \int_0^{n/\sqrt{2}} e^{-t^2} dt \qquad (1)$$

t is chosen to normalise the curve, and P is strictly increasing on n, so we are only required to find the largest z-score.

Calculating the z-score exactly can be quite costly, so we instead use the binomial approximation to the normal distribution with equal prior probabilities and find that a given z-score Z is:

$$Z = \frac{f - \mu}{\sigma} \qquad (2)$$

where f is the frequency count, μ is the mean in a pairwise test, and σ is the standard deviation of the test. A more complete derivation appears in Nicholson (2005).

3 Resources

We make use of a number of lexical resources in our implementation and evaluation. For corpus statistics, we use the written component of the BNC, a balanced 90M token corpus. To find verb–argument frequencies, we parse this using RASP (Briscoe and Carroll, 2002), a tag sequence grammar–based statistical parser. We contrast the corpus statistics with ones collected from the

Web, using an implementation of a freely available Google "scraper" from CPAN.[1]

For a given compound nominalisation, we wish to determine all possible verbal forms of the head. We do so using the combination of the morphological component of CELEX (Burnage, 1990), a lexical database, NOMLEX (Macleod et al., 1998), a nominalisation database, and CATVAR (Habash and Dorr, 2003), an automatically–constructed database of clusters of inflected words based on the Porter stemmer (Porter, 1997).

Once the verbal forms have been identified, we construct canonical forms of the present participle (*+ing*) and the past participle (*+ed*), using the morph lemmatiser (Minnen et al., 2001). We construct canonical forms of the plural head and plural modifier (*+s*) in the same manner.

For evaluation, we have the two–way classified data set used by Lapata (2002), and a three–way classified data set constructed from open text. Lapata automatically extracts candidates from the British National Corpus, and hand–curates a set of 796 compound nominalisations which were interpreted as either a subjective relation SUBJ (e.g. *wood appearance* "wood appears"), or a (direct) objective relation OBJ (e.g. *stress avoidance* "[SO] avoids stress". We automatically validated this data set for consistency, removing:

1. items that did not occur in the same chunk, according to a chunker based on fnTBL 1.0 (Ngai and Florian, 2001),
2. items whose head did not have a verbal form according to our lexical resources, and
3. items which consisted in part of proper nouns,

to end up with 695 consistent compounds. We used the method of Nicholson and Baldwin (2005) to derive a small data set of 129 compound nominalisations, also from the BNC, which we instructed three unskilled annotators to identify each as one of subjective (SUB), direct object (DOB), or prepositional object (POB, e.g. *side show* "[SO] show [ST] on the side"). The annotators identified nine prepositional relations: {about,against,for,from,in,into,on,to,with}.

[1] `www.cpan.org`: We limit our usage to examining the "Estimated Results Returned", so that our usage is identical to running the queries manually from the website. The Google API (`www.google.com/apis`) gives a method for examining the actual text of the returned documents.

4 Proposed Method

4.1 Paraphrase Tests

To derive preferences for the SUB, DOB, and various POB interpretations for a given compound nominalisation, the most obvious approach is to examine a parsed corpus for instances of the verbal form of the head and the modifier occurring in the corresponding verb–argument relation. There are other constructions that can be informative, however.

We examine two novel paraphrase tests: one prepositional and one participial. The prepositional test is based in part on the work by Leonard (1984) and Lauer (1995): for a given compound, we search for instances of the head and modifier nouns separated by a preposition. For example, for the compound nominalisation *leg operation*, we might search for *operation on the leg*, corresponding to the POB relation *on*. Special cases are *by*, corresponding to a subjective reading akin to a passive construction (e.g. *investor hesitancy, hesitancy by the investor* ≡ "the investor hesitates"), and *of*, corresponding to a direct object reading (e.g. *language speaker, speaker of the language* ≡ "[SO] speaks the language").

The participial test is based on the paraphrasing equivalence of using the present participle of the verbal head as an adjective before the modifier, for the SUB relation (e.g. *the hesitating investor* ≡ "the investor hesitates"), compared to the past participle for the DOB relation (*the spoken language* ≡ "[SO] speaks the language"). The corresponding prepositional object construction is unusual in English, but still possible: compare *?the operated-on leg* and *the lived-in village*.

4.2 The Algorithm

Given a compound nominalisation, we perform a number of steps to arrive at an interpretation. First, we derive a set of verbal forms for the head from the combination of CELEX, NOMLEX, and CATVAR. We find the participial forms of each of the verbal heads, and plurals for the nominal head and modifier, using the morph lemmatiser.

Next, we examine the BNC for instances of the modifier and one of the verbal head forms occurring in a verb–argument relation, with the aid of the RASP parse. Using these frequencies, we calculate the pairwise z-scores between SUB and DOB, and between SUB and POB: the score given to the SUB interpretation is the greater of the two.

We further examine the RASP parsed data for instances of the prepositional and participial tests for the compound, and calculate the z-scores for these as well.

We then collect our Google counts. Because the Web data is unparsed, we cannot look for syntactic structures explictly. Instead, we query a number of collocations which we expect to be representative of the desired structure.

For the prepositional test, the head can be singular or plural, the modifier can be singular or plural, and there may or may not be an article between the preposition and the modifier. For example, for the compound nominalisation *product replacement* and preposition *of* we search for all of the following: (and similarly for the other prepositions)

replacement of product
replacement of the product
replacement of products
replacement of the products
replacements of product
replacements of the product
replacements of products
replacements of the products

For the participial test, the modifier can be singular or plural, and if we are examining a prepositional relation, the head can be either a present or past participle. For *product replacement*, we search for, as well as other prepositions:

the replacing product
the replacing products
the replaced product
the replaced products
the replacing–about product
the replacing–about products
the replaced–about product
the replaced–about products

We comment briefly on these tests in Section 6.

We choose to use *the* as our canonical article because it is a reliable marker of the left boundary of an NP and number-neutral; using *a/an* represents a needless complication.

We then calculate the z-scores using the method described in Section 2, where the individual frequency counts are the maximum of the results obtained across the query set.

Once the z-scores have been obtained, we choose a classification based on the greatest-valued observed test. We contrast the confidence interval–based approach with the maximum likelihood method of choosing the largest of the raw frequencies. We also experiment with a machine learning package, to examine the mutual predictiveness of the separate tests.

5 Observed Results

First, we found majority-class baselines for each of the data sets. The two–way data set had 258 SUBJ–classified items, and 437 OBJ–classified items, so choosing OBJ each time gives a baseline of 62.9%. The three–way set had 22 SUB items, 63 of DOB, and 44 of POB, giving a baseline of 48.8%.

Contrasting this with human performance on the data set, Lapata recorded a raw inter-annotator agreement of 89.7% on her test set, which corresponds to a Kappa value $\kappa = 0.78$. On the three–way data set, three annotators had a agreement of 98.4% for identification and classification of observed compound nominalisations in open text, and $\kappa = 0.83$. For the three-way data set, the annotators were asked to both identify and classify compound nominalisations in free text, and agreement is thus calculated over all words in the test. The high agreement figure is due to the fact that most words could be trivially disregarded (e.g. were not nouns). Kappa corrects this for chance agreement, so we conclude that this task was still better-defined than the one posed by Lapata. One possible reason for this was the number of poorly–behaved compounds that we removed due to chunk inconsistencies, lack of a verbal form, or proper nouns: it would be difficult for the annotators to agree over compounds where an obvious well–defined interpretation was not available.

5.1 Comparison Classification

Results for classification over the Lapata two–way data set are given in Table 1, and results over the open data three–way set are given in Table 2. For these, we selected the greatest raw frequency count for a given test as the intended relation (Raw), or the greatest confidence interval according to the z-score (Z-Score). If a relation could not be selected due to ties (e.g., the scores were all 0), we selected the majority baseline. To deal with the nature of the two–way data set with respect to our three–way selection, we mapped compounds that we would prefer to be POB to OBJ, as there are

Paraphrase	Default	Corpus Counts		Web Counts	
		Raw	Z-Score	Raw	Z-Score
Verb–Argument	62.9	67.9	68.3	–	–
Prepositional	62.9	62.1	62.4	62.6	63.0
Participial	62.9	63.0	63.2	61.4	58.8

Table 1: Classification Results over the two–way data set, in %. Comparison of raw frequency counts vs. confidence–based z-scores, for BNC data and Google scrapings shown.

Paraphrase	Default	Corpus Counts		Web Counts	
		Raw	Z-Score	Raw	Z-Score
Verb–Argument	48.8	54.3	55.0	–	–
Prepositional	48.8	48.4	50.0	59.7	58.9
Participial	48.8	43.2	45.4	43.4	38.0

Table 2: Classification results over the three-way data set, in %. Comparison of raw frequency counts vs. confidence-based z-scores, for BNC data and Google scrapings shown.

compounds in the set (e.g. *adult provision*) that have a prepositional object reading ("provide for adults") but have been classified as a direct object OBJ.

The verb–argument counts obtained from the parsed BNC are significantly better than the baseline for the Lapata data set ($\chi^2 = 4.12, p \leq 0.05$), but not significantly better for the open data set ($\chi^2 = 0.99, p \leq 1$). Similar results were reported by Lapata (2002) over her data set using backed–off smoothing, the most closely related method.

Neither the prepositional nor participial paraphrases were significantly better than the baseline for either the two–way ($\chi^2 = 0.00, p \leq 1$), or the three–way data set ($\chi^2 = 3.52, p \leq 0.10$), although the prepositional test did slightly improve on the verb–argument results.

5.2 Machine Learning Classification

Although the results were not impressive, we still believed that there was complementing information within the data, which could be extracted with the aid of a machine learner. For this, we made use of TiMBL (Daelemans et al., 2003), a nearest-neighbour classifier which stores the entire training set and extrapolates further samples, as a principled method for combination of the data. We use TiMBL's in-built cross-validation method: 90% of the data set is used as training data to test the other 10%, for each stratified tenth of the set. The results it achieves are assumed to be able to generalise to new samples if they are compared to the current training data set.

The results observed using TiMBL are shown in Table 3. This was from the combination of all of the available paraphrase tests: verb–argument, prepositional, and participial for the corpus counts, and just prepositional and participial for the Web counts. The results for the two–way data set derived from Lapata's data set were a good improvement over the simple classification results, significantly so for the Web frequencies ($\chi^2 = 20.3, p \leq 0.01$). However, we also notice a corresponding decrease in the results for the three–way open data set, which make these improvements immaterial.

	Corpus Counts	Web Counts
Two–way Set	72.4	74.2
Three–way Set	51.1	50.4

Table 3: TiMBL results for the combination of paraphrase tests over the two–way and three–way data sets for corpus and Web frequencies

Examining the other possible combinations for the tests did indeed lead to varying results, but not in a consistent manner. For example, the best combination for the open data set was using the participial raw scores and z-scores (58.1%), which performed particularly badly in simple comparisons, and comparatively poorly (70.2%) for the two–way set.

6 Discussion

Although the observed results failed to match, or even approach, various benchmarks set by Lapata (2002) (87.3% accuracy) and Grover et al. (2005) (77%) for the subject–object and subject–

direct object–prepositional objects classification tasks respectively, the presented approach is not without merit. Indeed, these results relied on machine learning approaches incorporating many features independent of corpus counts: namely, context, suffix information, and semantic similarity resources. Our results were an examination of the possible contribution of lexical information available from high–volume unparsed text.

One important concept used in the above benchmarks was that of statistical smoothing, both class–based and distance–based. The reason for this is the inherent data sparseness within the corpus statistics for these paraphrase tests. Lapata (2002) observes that almost half (47%) of the verb–noun pairs constructed are not attested within the BNC. Grover et al. (2005) also note the sparseness of observed relations. Using the immense data source of the Web allows one to circumvent this problem: only one compound (*anarchist prohibition*) has no instances of the paraphrases from the scraping,[2] from more than 900 compounds between the two data sets. This extra information, we surmise, would be beneficial for the smoothing procedures, as the comparative accuracy between the two methods is similar.

On the other hand, we also observe that simply alleviating the data sparseness is insufficient to provide a reliable interpretation. These results reinforce the contribution made by the statistical and semantic resources used in arriving at these benchmarks.

The approach suggested by Keller and Lapata (2003) for obtaining bigram information from the Web could provide an approach for estimating the syntactic verb–argument counts for a given compound (dashes in Tables 1 and 2). In spite of the inherent unreliability of approximating long–range dependencies with n-gram information, results look promising. An examination of the effectiveness of this approach is left as further research. Similarly, various methods of combining corpus counts with the Web counts, including smoothing, backing–off, and machine learning, could also lead to interesting performance impacts.

Another item of interest is the comparative difficulty of the task presented by the three–way data set extracted from open data, and the two–way data set hand–curated by Lapata. The baseline of this set is much lower, even compared that of the similar task (albeit domain–specific) from Grover et al. (2005) of 58.6%. We posit that the hand–filtering of the data set in these works contributes to a biased sample. For example, removing prepositional objects for a two–way classification, which make up about a third of the open data set, renders the task somewhat artificial.

Comparison of the results between the maximum likelihood estimates used in earlier work, and the more statistically robust confidence intervals were inconclusive as to performance improvement, and were most effective as a feature expansion algorithm. The only obvious result is an aesthetic one, in using "robust statistics".

Finally, the paraphrase tests which we propose are not without drawbacks. In the prepositional test, a paraphrase with *of* does not strictly contribute to a direct object reading: consider *school aim* "school aims", for which instances of *aim by the school* are overwhelmed by *aim of the school*. We experimented with permutations of the available queries (e.g. requiring the head and modifier to be of different number, to reflect the pluralisability of the head in such compounds, e.g. *aims of the school*), without observing substantially different results.

Another observation is the inherent bias of the prepositional test to the prepositional object relation. Apparent prepositional relations can occur in spite of the available verb frames: consider *cash limitation*, where the most populous instance is *limitation on cash*, despite the impossibility of **to limit on cash* (for *to place a limit on cash*). Another example, is *bank agreement*: finding instances of *agreement with bank* does not lead to the pragmatically absurd [SO] *agrees with the bank*.

Correspondingly, the participial relation has the opposite bias: constructions of the form *the lived-in flat* "[SO] lived in the flat" are usually lexicalised in English. As such, only 17% of compounds in the two–way data set and 34% of the three-way data set display non-zero values in the prepositional object relation for the participial test. We hoped that the inherent biases of the two tests might balance each other, but there is little evidence of that from the results.

[2] Interestingly, Google only lists 3 occurrences of this compound anyway, so token relevance is low — further inspection shows that those 3 are not well-formed in any case.

7 Conclusion

We presented two novel paraphrase tests for automatically predicting the inherent semantic relation of a given compound nominalisation as one of subject, direct object, or prepositional object. We compared these to the usual verb–argument paraphrase test, using corpus statistics, and frequencies obtained by scraping the Google search engine. We also implemented a more robust statistical measure than the insipid maximum likelihood estimates — the confidence interval. A significant reduction in data sparseness was achieved, but this alone is insufficient to provide a substantial performance improvement.

Acknowledgements

We would like to thank the members of the University of Melbourne LT group and the three anonymous reviewers for their valuable input on this research, as well as Mirella Lapata for allowing use of the data.

References

Ted Briscoe and John Carroll. 2002. Robust accurate statistical annotation of general text. In *Proceedings of the 3rd International Conference on Language Resources and Evaluation*, pages 1499–1504, Las Palmas, Canary Islands.

Gavin Burnage. 1990. CELEX: A guide for users. Technical report, University of Nijmegen.

Lou Burnard. 2000. *User Reference Guide for the British National Corpus*. Technical report, Oxford University Computing Services.

Walter Daelemans, Jakub Zavrel, Ko van der Sloot, and Antal van den Bosch. 2003. *TiMBL: Tilburg Memory Based Learner, version 5.0, Reference Guide*. ILK Technical Report 03-10.

Tim Finin. 1980. The semantic interpretation of nominal compounds. In *Proceedings of the First National Conference on Artificial Intelligence*, pages 310–315, Stanford, USA. AAAI Press.

Gregory Grefenstette. 1998. The World Wide Web as a resource for example-based machine translation tasks. In *Proceedings of the ASLIB Conference on Translating and the Computer*, London, UK.

Claire Grover, Mirella Lapata, and Alex Lascarides. 2005. A comparison of parsing technologies for the biomedical domain. *Journal of Natural Language Engineering*, 11(01):27–65.

Nizar Habash and Bonnie Dorr. 2003. A categorial variation database for English. In *Proceedings of the 2003 Human Language Technology Conference of the North American Chapter of the ACL*, pages 17–23, Edmonton, Canada.

Pierre Isabelle. 1984. Another look at nominal compounds. In *Proceeedings of the 10th International Conference on Computational Linguistics and 22nd Annual Meeting of the ACL*, pages 509–516, Stanford, USA.

Bernard Jones. 1995. Predicating nominal compounds. In *Proceedings of the 17th International Conference of the Cognitive Science Society*, pages 130–5, Pittsburgh, USA.

Frank Keller and Mirella Lapata. 2003. Using the web to obtain frequencies for unseen bigrams. *Computational Linguistics*, 29(3):459–484.

John F. Kenney and E. S. Keeping, 1962. *Mathematics of Statistics, Pt. 1*, chapter 11.4, pages 167–9. Van Nostrand, Princeton, USA, 3rd edition.

Mirella Lapata and Frank Keller. 2005. Web-based models for natural language processing. *ACM Transactions on Speech and Language Processing*, 2(1).

Mirella Lapata and Alex Lascarides. 2003. Detecting novel compounds: The role of distributional evidence. In *Proceedings of the 10th Conference of the European Chapter of the Association for Computional Linguistics*, pages 235–242, Budapest, Hungary.

Maria Lapata. 2002. The disambiguation of nominalizations. *Computational Linguistics*, 28(3):357–388.

Mark Lauer. 1995. *Designing Statistical Language Learners: Experiments on Noun Compounds*. Ph.D. thesis, Macquarie University, Sydney, Australia.

Rosemary Leonard. 1984. *The Interpretation of English Noun Sequences on the Computer*. Elsevier Science, Amsterdam, the Netherlands.

Judith Levi. 1978. *The Syntax and Semantics of Complex Nominals*. Academic Press, New York, USA.

Beth Levin. 1993. *English Verb Classes and Alternations*. The University of Chicago Press, Chicago, USA.

Catherine Macleod, Ralph Grishman, Adam Meyers, Leslie Barrett, and Ruth Reeves. 1998. NOMLEX: A lexicon of nominalizations. In *Proceedings of the 8th International Congress of the European Association for Lexicography*, pages 187–193, Liege, Belgium.

Guido Minnen, John Carroll, and Darren Pearce. 2001. Applied morphological processing of English. *Natural Language Engineering*, 7(3):207–23.

Preslov Nakov and Marti Hearst. 2005. Search engine statistics beyond the n-gram: Application to noun compound bracketing. In *Proceedings of the Ninth Conference on Computational Natural Language Learning*, pages 17–24, Ann Arbor, USA.

Grace Ngai and Radu Florian. 2001. Transformation-based learning in the fast lane. In *Proceedings of the 2nd Annual Meeting of the North American Chapter of the Association for Computational Linguistics*, pages 40–7, Pittsburgh, USA.

Jeremy Nicholson and Timothy Baldwin. 2005. Statistical interpretation of compound nominalisations. In *Proceeding of the Australasian Langugae Technology Workshop 2005*, Sydney, Australia.

Jeremy Nicholson. 2005. Statistical interpretation of compound nouns. Honours Thesis, University of Melbourne, Melbourne, Australia.

Martin Porter. 1997. An algorithm for suffix stripping. In Karen Sparck Jones and Peter Willett, editors, *Readings in information retrieval*. Morgan Kaufmann, San Francisco, USA.

Barbara Rosario and Marti Hearst. 2001. Classifying the semantic relations in noun compounds via a domain-specific lexical hierarchy. In *Proceedings of the 6th Conference on Empirical Methods in Natural Language Processing*, Pittsburgh, USA.

Takaaki Tanaka and Timothy Baldwin. 2003. Noun-noun compound machine translation: A feasibility study on shallow processing. In *Proceedings of the ACL 2003 Workshop on Multiword Expressions: Analysis, Acquisition and Treatment*, pages 17–24, Sapporo, Japan.

Lucy Vanderwende. 1994. Algorithm for automatic interpretation of noun sequences. In *Proceedings of the 15th International Conference on Computational Linguistics*, pages 782–788, Kyoto, Japan.

Beatrice Warren. 1978. *Semantic Patterns of Noun-Noun Compounds*. Acta Universitatis Gothoburgensis, Göteborg, Sweden.

Xiaojin Zhu and Ronald Rosenfeld. 2001. Improving trigram language modeling with the World Wide Web. In *Proceedings of the International Conference on Acoustics, Speech, and Signal Processing*, pages 533–6, Salt Lake City, USA.

Author Index

Association for Computational Linguistics
209 N. Eighth Street
Stroudsburg, Pennsylvania 18360